CASS ABRAHAMS
Cooks Cape Malay

Food from Africa

To my husband, Jowa, and my children Rehane, Shakira and Zaid, for all the joy you bring me and for all your patience and hardy stomachs when called to taste my many "creations".

CASS ABRAHAMS
Cooks Cape Malay

Food from Africa

METZ PRESS

Author's Acknowledgements
The author would like to thank Elsa van der Nest for making available her premises for the cover photograph, as well as the following for their kindness and generosity in supplying props for the food photography:
LIM, Banks, The Yellow Door, Peter Visser Interiors and Spirit

And to my publisher, Wilsia Metz, thank you for not getting a nervous breakdown when trying to cope with my handling of deadlines.

Published by Metz Press
Unit 107, Hoheizen Park 1
Hoheizen Crescent
Hoheizen 7530

Conversion table: Liquid capacity

Metric	Imperial equivalent
25 ml	1 fluid oz
50 ml	2 fluid oz
100 ml	4 fluid oz
150 ml	5 fluid oz
300 ml	10 fluid oz
500 ml	17 fluid oz
600 ml	20 fluid oz/1 pint
1 litre	35 fluid oz

First published in 1995
Second impression 1996
Second edition 2000
Copyright © Metz Press
Text © Cass Abrahams
Foreword © Dr M Cassiem D'Arcy
Food photography © Cass Abrahams
Cultural photographs © Shafiq Morton pp. 26, 33, 36, 39, 42, 46, 52, 57, 61, 66, 74, 78, 84, 92, 94, 95
George Hallet pp. 16, 44, 53, 55, 58, 88 and contents page

Reproduction of original watercolour from the District Six collection by John Hall page 7 courtesy of Jowa Abrahams. Cultural photograph on page 92 courtesy of the South African National Gallery

Editor and coordinator: Wilsia Metz
Designer: Julie Farquhar, Ink Design, Zeekoevlei
Repro and print coordinator: Andrew de Kock, Table View
Food photography: Brandon Amron-Coetzee, Cape Town
Food styling: Justine Drake, Mowbray
Reproduction: Cape Imaging Bureau, Gardens
Printing and binding: Tien Wah Press (Pte) Limited, Singapore

ISBN 1-875001-44-1

CONTENTS

FOREWORD

Bobotie, Yellow Rice, Sosaties and Peach Pickles are noted as South Africa's official entries in the *United Nations Cookbook* of 1967. All of these delectable dishes come from the dining table of the Cape Malays. Who are the Cape Malays and why is their cuisine so favoured by South African palates?

In the mid-seventeenth century the Dutch East India Company needed a midway refreshment station on the long sea-route between Holland and the spice-rich East Indies. Jan van Riebeeck was sent to the Cape of Good Hope as the settlement's first commander and given the mission to erect a hospital, establish a garden and provide food for passing ships. He built a fort on what is now the Grand Parade in Cape Town and constructed the Company Gardens on the site of the present Cape Town Gardens.

This intrusion into their territory incurred the wrath of the indigenous Khoisan peoples.

War was inevitable. To protect the fort and the newly-found settlement, Van Riebeeck requested help from the Here XVII, the senior officials of the Dutch East India Company in Batavia.

They sent the Mardijkers, soldiers of fortune from the East Indian island of Amboina, to the Cape in 1658. Given their Eastern origin, one may surmise that the Mardijkers were probably the first to bring the flavourful East Indian dishes we know so well to these shores.

But furthermore, the Dutch, fuelled by a craving to secure the monopoly of the lucrative spice trade between the East and Europe, expanded their forrays into the spice islands during the seventeenth century, relentlessly destroying the old kingdoms in what is now known as Indonesia.

They also fought and defeated their great rivals, the Portuguese, and Malacca, the biggest port on the Malay peninsula, fell into Dutch hands.

The Dutch East India Company established many trading posts on the Indian subcontinent, from the Bay of Bengal in the north down south to the Malabar and Coromandel coasts.

It was from these outposts in India, Malaya and Indonesia that the Dutch brought political exiles and highly-skilled slaves to the Cape to build and secure the prosperity of their colony at the southern tip of Africa. 'Malay' slaves were highly prized and expensive, employed almost exclusively in skilled positions as artisans, fishermen, seamstresses and cooks in the homes of the wealthy Cape Burghers.

The Cape's distinctive architecture to this day attests to their skills and craftsmanship.

The Cape Malays intermarried with all the races that drifted through the colony: settlers who came from Madagascar, Mozambique, Angola and all the European nations. But through the years, because of their staunch Muslim faith, they remained a distinct entity, following a rich culture: a colourful amalgam between their languid eastern heritage and the all-engulfing, clinical, pragmatic west.

Their *moppies* (humorous ditties) sing of love won, love lost, but above all, they serenade an almost divine love for food.

From birth till death the Cape Malays celebrate each and every occasion with groaning tables bedecked with the bounteous fruits of the earth and the labour of a thousand kitchen fingers, each dish suffused with wondrous spices from their far-off ancestral islands.

Nowhere on earth are there people who relish a feast so much as the Cape Malays; nowhere on this planet is there a community so fervent in thanks to the Almighty for the blessings of the table.

Culture and cuisine are evolutionary, changing with the seasons, with the tides of history.

The recipes in this book are delectable, nurtured and coddled by a cook with a velvet touch for good food, one inspired and propelled by an undying urge to caress the public palate with the subtle, sensuous titillations of Cape Malay cooking.

Cashifa (Cass) Abrahams has tested, tried and modified the dishes to suit the modest pocket, the modern table, the gourmet, the lover, the poet. She has kept an eye on the preservation of the Cape Malay culinary tradition, the Islamic heritage, yet moved with the times.

But, wait ... I smell something. Go ahead. Sniff. Hmmm! The restaurants and Cape byways are redolent

TENNANT STREET, DISTRICT SIX.

with a thousand and one spicy fragrances ... the tables sway, loaded with a thousand and one steaming Indo-Malay dishes.

There's Sosaties and Bobotie, Samoosas and Beryani, Slamse Kerrie and Gesmoorde Rys, Denningvleis with Sambals, Sweet Yellow Rice and Plaatfrikkadelle, Gesmoorde Snoek, Pickala, Waterblommetjies with Surings, ony-ony, koeksisters, puddings and pies and Falooda to quench the thirst. My mouth drools, my stomach groans ...

Before I say *Bismillah*, I go on my knees and pray that Cape Malay cuisine will have a firm foothold in our national culinary tradition for aeons to come.

Congratulations, Cass; keep the cooking pots bubbling and the ovens going. When we pat our cellulite and our paunches we'll salute you.

M. Cassiem D'Arcy

FOOD & TRADITION

Food plays an important role in the Cape Malay community and is always central to their colourful religious and family feasts. There is an old Javanese tradition which says 'It is not sufficient that a man should place good food before his guest; he is bound to do more. He should render the meal palatable by kind words of treatment, to soothe him after his journey and to make his heart glad while he partakes of refreshment' (T S Rafles: *The History of Java*). This tradition is accurately reflected in the lives of the Cape Malays who are known for their warm hospitality that knows no bounds of race or status. They are courteous, attentive and entertaining hosts. When a Muslim invites guests he expresses a *niyyat*, or intention, to have a feast. After these feasts people are often seen to wrap leftovers in serviettes to take home with them. This, unlike in Western culture, is not considered rude or impolite, for once the *niyyat* is made, the food no longer belongs to the host, but to the guests whom the host intended to entertain. After any feast in the community large amounts of leftovers are also taken to old-age homes and orphanages, or distributed among the 'Bergies' who descend in droves whenever a feast or wedding is celebrated. (They seem to have a very effective information network – it does not take long for the hoards of homeless to gather at the kitchen entrances of the many venues where special celebrations take place.)

FOOD IN THE HOME

In the Cape Malay home the main meal is served in the evening when the head of the household returns from work, except on a Friday when the men go to the mosque for the compulsory noon *Ju'maah* congregational prayer service, and return to a spread cooked by their wives. The Sunday midday meal is also important as all the members of the family are together and guests often pop in for a visit and join the family for a meal. Any person who is in the house at meal time will be invited to eat from the table of the host as it is believed that every person who eats from his table bestows a *barakat*, or blessing, on his home, thus ensuring that his home will never be without food. It is considered very impolite for a guest to refuse the invitation.

Food is never counted or weighed off into exact portions for the family as one must always cater for the unexpected guest. It is a great shame when there is not enough food to serve everyone at the table. When unexpected visitors arrive and the hostess realizes that she does not have enough food for everyone, she will go out of her way to prepare extra food in no time.

In the Cape Malay tradition such a dish, quick and easy to prepare, consists of simple ingredients out of the kitchen cupboard and is called a *stappie* or a *smoortjie*. Food is never plated by the hostess as it is impossible for her to know how much each person wants to eat. Plates must always be cleared since it is believed that throwing away food is tantamount to throwing away your luck.

Traditionally, a meal in a Cape Malay home is not served as courses. Instead, a large variety of dishes is placed on the table and guests help themselves to whatever they prefer. Children are taught to place a small helping of a particular dish on their plates at a time, to eat this and then dish up a little of the next dish until they have had sufficient to eat. This ensures that the flavours of the various dishes, each with its own unique combination of spices, do not mix. The mother of the house, or the hostess, very rarely sits down to eat at the table. She will ensure that the containers remain filled with hot food, and sees to the comfort and well-being of everyone around the table.

Before every meal Bismillah is said. This means '*In the name of Allah*'. In accordance with ancient tradition the host will serve himself first, and then the senior male guests. Besides soup and certain puddings, food is eaten with the fingers of the right hand in such a way that the palm of the hand never gets dirty.

Each guest is given a jammerlappie, a wet cloth, to cleanse the fingers and remove any crumbs from the lips. Guests are given the opportunity to wash their hands before and after the meal, and to rinse their mouths. When Western guests are invited for a meal, the table is set with knives and forks to accommodate them, but the fork is always placed on the right-hand side. Food must never be brought to the mouth with the left hand which is used to cleanse the body orifices.

Halaal and haraam

The teachings of Islam, the religion practised by most Cape Malays, dictate which foods may be eaten. Whatever is permissible is said to be *halaal*, while everything forbidden is *haraam*. Only *halaal* meat may be consumed.

Animals must be slaughtered in accordance with Islamic rules: they must be blemish-free and healthy, and the words *'In the name of Allah'*, *'Allah the Almighty'* and *'Allah is great'* must be intoned during the slaughtering.

For meat to be halaal the animal must be killed with a single stroke of a sharp blade. If the animal suffers in any way the meat becomes *haraam*. Consuming blood is *haraam*, and after slaughtering the animal is left to bleed until white. Before any meat is cooked, it is washed thoroughly in water to remove all traces of blood. Hence the reference to 'wet meat' in traditional Cape Malay recipes.

Pork is *haraam* to all Muslims. If meat is transported in a truck which previously transported pork, or kept in a refrigerator with pork or placed in any container in which pork was kept, such meat also becomes haraam.

Alcohol or any intoxicating substance is strictly *haraam*. A Muslim may not drink, sell or serve any alcohol. Instead, an interesting variety of fruit punches, milk-based beverages or tea is offered. Food cooked in alcohol is also forbidden even though all the alcohol evaporates during the cooking process.

Fish and seafood

Seafood is *halaal*. I always advise non-Muslims wishing to invite Muslims for a meal to serve fish. Because the Western Cape is surrounded by the sea, fish has always been a firm favourite in the Cape Malay community. There are many fishermen and fish vendors among the Cape Malays and in earlier times the plaintive cry of the fish-horn used to draw women out daily to buy fresh fish from the fish vendor.

Fish and shellfish are prepared in interesting and exciting ways. A firm favourite is snoek: dried, smoked, pickled or used in stews and curries. A famous saying in the Cape Malay community is: 'If you have snoek in the house, you have food on the table.'

Unless used in an exotic dish, such as crayfish curry, fish is rarely served on Sundays or for special celebrations as it is considered huiskos. It is often served on Mondays after Sunday's rich meal.

Motjie-kok

A good cook or *motjie-kok* is highly regarded in the community and is often asked to cook for weddings and funerals where she presides in unquestioning glory. She usually has a team of women who will clean, fetch and carry while she cooks, often for more than 1 000 guests. When food is prepared for such big crowds, the cooking is often done outside on an open fire in huge containers – the demands of the characteristic Cape Malay hospitality often exceed the capacity of conventional kitchens and stoves.

No money is charged for the services of a *motjie-kok*, but it is understood that if ever she requires any favour from a family she has assisted, she will be accommodated. This custom dates back to the days of the slaves when they would exchange services.

This is known as *kanala werk* and the custom is still practised today.

A builder would build your house over week-ends in return for which you, if you happen to be a teacher, would coach his children in difficult school subjects, or, if you happen to be a good cook, cook for his daughter's wedding reception.

Keeping it in the family

Recipes are handed down from generation to generation and are highly prized. The Cape Malays cook most of their dishes the same way their forefathers did almost 300 years ago. Their recipes are jealously guarded as families like to be known as the best pastry makers, or the best Beryani makers or the best Bobotie makers in the community. When an outsider requests a recipe it is often given with an essential ingredient or step missing.

When the slaves were liberated they acquired land in the areas where they worked. Slaves from Bishops Court settled in Claremont and those working in Constantia settled in the neigbourhood.

Most of the Cape Malays who lived in Cape Town and the Bo-Kaap were free burghers. Because of the distance between Constantia and Claremont, and Cape town where the spices were obtained, cooks in the Claremont and Constantia area adapted their recipes to the availability of the ingredients.

While researching this book I came across various different recipes for what is basically the same dish – the flavour of the foodand the combination of spices often tells from which area the cook comes.

mustard seed

ground mace

fennel

cinnamon sticks

USING AND STORING SPICES

Roast whole spices in an oven to intensify the flavour and grind finely. I have a special coffee grinder which I find most effective for this purpose. Ground spices have a shorter shelf-life than whole spices – they normally don't retain their flavour for much longer than one to three months – and should always be purchased in small quantities.

Always store spices in an airtight container, preferably in a cool space.

garlic

SPICES & HERBS

nutmeg

mace

cloves

Spices are essential to Cape Malay cuisine where it is combined masterfully in many different ways to create the most interesting variety of flavours and aromas. For centuries obtaining spices involved an immense effort. Today most spices are readily available from supermarkets or specialist shops. Some knowledge of the different aromas and flavours imparted by various spices is imported in order to use and combine them with maximum effect. The spices we use today come from the fruit, seed, bark or root of a variety of plants. The quantities and combinations of spices used in various dishes impart the specific flavour of each dish. The following spices and herbs are used most often in Cape Malay cuisine:

ALLSPICE (PIMENTO) (*Enginia acris*)
Sunripe, sun-dried berries of the pimento tree which grows in the Caribbean. It tastes like a combination of pepper, cloves, cinnamon and nutmeg, hénce the name *wonderpeper* (wonder pepper) in Afrikaans. Allspice is an essential ingredient in many Cape Malay dishes.

ANISEED (*Pimpinella anisum*)
The seeds of the anise plant, which produces clusters of yellow-white flowers, have a sweetish liquorice flavour and are used mainly in cakes and confectionery. Use sparingly as the flavour can be overpowering.

BAY LEAVES (*Laurus nobilis*)
Come from the evergreen bay or laurel tree. Also known as laurel, the leaves are used fresh or dried. Bay leaves are used mainly in dishes with an acidic flavour, such as pickled fish, pienang curry and some bredies.

CARDAMOM (*Elettaria cardamomum*)
An expensive spice, sometimes called the seed of paradise. The fruit is harvested before it is completely ripe, and carefully dried to prevent the pod from bursting and releasing its 17-20 small, black seeds. The seeds have a wonderful aroma which enhances the flavour of curries and desserts alike. It is normally used whole for food and ground for desserts and cakes.

CASSIA (*Cinnamomum cassia*)
The bark of the cassia is similar to that of the cinnamon tree, but less fragrant. It has a sharp, pungent flavour and is used extensively in curries.

CINNAMON (*Cinnamomum zeylanicum*)
The bark of the cinnamon tree has a delicate, aromatic fragrance and is sweeter than cassia. Cinnamon is used in desserts, cakes and preserves, but is inclined to spoil a curry.

saffron

tamarind

curry leaves

turmeric

GHARUM MASALA
Makes 750 g (1 ¹/₂ lb)

15 g (¹/₂ oz) cardamom pods
500 g (18 oz) coriander seeds
125 g (5 oz) cumin seeds
30 g (1 oz) cloves
60 g (2 oz) black peppercorns
30 g (2 oz) cinnamon sticks
1 nutmeg

Intensify flavours of seeds by roasting in an oven at 180°C/350°F until lightly toasted. Grind and keep in an airtight container to use as required.

ground coriander

coriander seeds

star aniseed

black peppercorns

green root ginger

CHILLIES (*Capsicum spp.*)
There are many different varieties, used sparingly in Cape Malay cuisine where the emphasis is on the interplay of spices rather than sharpness. Chillies are used in sambals accompanying dishes which require sharpness. Dried chillies form an essential ingredient of masala.

CLOVES (*Eugenia aromatica*)
The unopened flower buds of an evergreen tree found in Mauritius, Zanzibar, Madagascar and the Philippines. The buds are picked when red, and sun-dried until they are a darkish brown colour. Cloves are used in curries and impart a delicious flavour to beryanis and bredies.

CORIANDER (*Coriandrum sativum*)
Also known as dhania, both the fresh leaves and the dried seeds are used extensively in curries. Fresh coriander leaves chopped and sprinkled over food enhance the flavour and look attractive. Dried seeds are ground and used in curry dishes. Coriander also enhances the flavour of pickled fish and meat.

CUMIN (*Cuminum cyminum*)
Also known as jeera, the seeds resemble caraway seeds, but the flavour differs completely. Seeds are dried and used whole or ground in various curries. Chewing cumin seeds freshens the breath after a spicy meal.

CURRY LEAVES (*Hypericum revolutum*)
Come from the curry bush which is related to the lemon tree. They have a distinct curry odour and impart a lemony flavour. Curry leaves are used fresh or dried, often together with masala.

FENNEL (*Foeniculum vulgare*)
Also known as barishap, it has a sweet liquorice flavour similar to that of dill. It's often used in delicate chicken and fish curries. Only the seeds are used; never the bulbs. An an essential ingredient of gharum masala.

FENUGREEK (*Trigonella foenum-graecum*)
Also known as methi, the seed is extremely hard and has to be heated to release its delicious aroma and flavour. It is used in atjars, pickles and some curries, but sparingly as it gives a sweet and sharp flavour.

GARLIC (*Allium sativum*)
As flavouring, garlic is used more sparingly in Cape Malay than in Indian curries. The flavour of fresh garlic differs significantly from that of dried. Most Cape Malay recipes require fresh rather than dried garlic which may impart an acrid, bitter flavour.

GINGER (*Zingiber officinale*)
Grown in India, china and Jamaica. The underground stem of the plant is used, peeled before being crushed or sliced, and has an aromatic, biting and slightly sweet taste. When ginger is dried and ground its

Masala
Makes 800 g (28 oz)

100 g (4 oz) dried red chillies
50 g (2 oz) black peppercorns
250 g (8 oz) cumin seeds
300 g (10 oz) coriander seeds
50 g (2 oz) turmeric
50 g (2 oz) ground ginger
10 g (¹/₂ oz) cloves
10 g (¹/₂ oz) cinnamon sticks
5 g (¹/₅ oz) cardamom pods

Intensify the flavours of the seeds by roasting them in an oven at 180°C/350°F for a few minutes. Grind and mix with ground spices. Store prepared masala in an airtight container to use as required.

whole allspice

fenugreek

aniseed

coarsely ground red chilli

green chilli

bay leaves

cardamom pods

cassia sticks

cumin seeds

ground cumin

flavour changes significantly. It is indispensable for curries. It is also used in sweet dishes and preserves.

Mustard Seed (*Brassica spp.*)
Comes from several species of a Eurasian plant family. The seeds may be used whole or powdered. Whole seeds are use for masala, and added to pickles and atjars.

Naartjie Peel or Satsuma Orange
Dried naartjie peel is used by most Cape Malay cooks, whole or crushed into a fine powder, mainly in sweet dishes, or to give rice a special flavour. It is essential for traditional koeksisters.

Nutmeg and Mace (*Myristica fragrans*)
Although apparently so different, they belong to the same plant. Nutmeg is the seed while mace is its red covering. Both are used extensively, especially in puddings and bredies. Nutmeg also enhances the flavour of frikkadels.

Pepper (*Piper nigrum*)
Grown in the East Indian forests. Black pepper comes from the fruit, complete in its dark, black shell, while pepper is made from the ripe berries from which the dark shell had been removed. Pepper is one of our most important spices, imparting a sharp, warm taste to many dishes. Use whole in curries and whole and ground in bredies.

Saffron (*Crocus sativus*)
The most expensive spice in use today as it takes the stamens of 75 000 flowers to produce a mere 450 g (1 lb) of dried saffron. It has a penetrating taste and gives food a warm yellow colour. It is used sparingly in dishes cooked for feasts and weddings. No beryani is complete without a sprinkling of saffron.

Tamarind (*Tamarindis indica*)
The pasty, dried fruit of an Indian tree, used to give an acidic flavour to curries or stews. It is more aromatic and spicier than vinegar which may be used as a substitute. Tamarind is an essential ingredient for an authentic fish of crayfish curry.

Turmeric (*Curcuma longa*)
Comes from an East Indian plant and is a member of the ginger family. Its underground stem is dried and ground and used to add a yellow tint to curries. It may be used as a substitute for saffron, but sparingly as it tends to make food bitter.

Don't be filled with trepidation when you encounter spices, but do as the kitchen slaves of old when they added them to the food of their Dutch masters with free abandon and created South African cuisine as we know it.

HUISKOS

Rice is one of the most important dishes on the Cape Malay table. Although it is served in many different forms at feasts and celebrations, rice food, or *huiskos*, is traditionally regarded as every-day food. Rice is the staple food of the Cape Malay and is served at least once a day with the main meal. In fact, any meal served without rice is considered snack food. When cooked the Cape Malay way, rice must be loose and fluffy. It is interesting to note that older historic records contain references to 'the half-cooked rice boiled by the slaves'. The Malay slaves followed a method of cooking rice which was unknown to the European settlers. They have always considered the correct cooking of rice important – not mushy but every grain separate.

Rice forms an essential ingredient of the popular Beryanis and is served with a great variety of meat, poultry and fish dishes. Yellow rice made with saffron is served for special celebrations. Other popular traditional Cape Malay rice dishes include sweet saffron rice, coconut rice, spicy rice served with curries, almond rice, rice pudding and a rice cake known as *Kolwadjib*.

Most of the rice enjoyed at South African tables is imported from America and Thailand. A small quantity of high quality white rice is also imported from Pakistan. This is a long-grained white rice known as Basmati – the most prized rice in the Cape Malay community. It fills the kitchen with the most wonderful aroma while being cooked and it takes a skilled cook to get the rice grains loose and fluffy.

Rice also has important cultural uses. When a Cape Malay woman moves into a new house, the first items she carries with her over the threshold are three small containers, one filled with rice, one with sugar and one with salt. These containers are placed in the back of a kitchen cupboard where they stay until the family moves. The rice ensures that her cupboards will never be empty, the sugar that the household will be filled with sweetness, and the salt keeps away evil spirits.

During the fast of Ramadan anyone who is too old or too ill to fast must pay a penalty to the poor in the form of four cups of rice per day, or the equivalent in money.

Bredies are commonplace on the Cape Malay table and together with curries, form the bulk of *huiskos*. Louis Leipoldt's description of a bredie is one of the best I've ever come across. He says: '[Bredies] are a combination of meat and vegetables so intimately stewed that the flesh is thoroughly impregnated with the vegetable flavour while the vegetables have benefited from the meat fluids ... neither dominates but both combine to make a delectable whole that is a triumph of cooperative achievement ...' (*Leipoldt's Cape Cookery* C Louis Leipoldt). The meat constituent should be deliciously tender and wholly in sympathy with the main vegetable.

TOMATO BREDIE

2 large onions, sliced
2 ml (1/2 tsp) peppercorns
2 ml (1/2 tsp) ground cloves
125 ml (1/2 cup) water
25 ml (2 tbsp) vegetable oil
2 sticks cinnamon
1 kg (2¼ lb) mutton
3 cm fresh root ginger, finely chopped
2 cardamom pods
1 kg (2¼ lb) ripe tomatoes, chopped or
3 cans (410 g/14 oz) chopped tomatoes
1 green chilli, chopped
medium potatoes, peeled and halved
salt, pepper and sugar to taste
chopped parsley for garnishing

Few bredies are more delicious than this firm favourite, always best with fresh, very ripe tomatoes. Chicken may be used instead of mutton, but then the cooking time must be reduced. Serves 8

Place onions, peppercorns, cloves and water in a large saucepan and bring to the boil. Simmer until all the water has been absorbed. Add oil and cinnamon and braise until onions are golden.

Add meat, ginger and cardamom pods and stir thoroughly. Turn down the heat, cover saucepan with a tightly-fitting lid and simmer gently for 30 minutes. Add tomatoes and chilli. Close lid and simmer for 20 minutes.

Now add potatoes, salt, freshly ground pepper and sugar to taste. Replace lid and simmer until potatoes are cooked.

Garnish with chopped parsley and serve with samp and beans (*see* page 21) or on a bed of freshly-cooked rice.

GREEN-BEAN BREDIE

Always popular, this green-bean bredie has its own distinct combination of flavours. Serves 8

Boil onions, cloves, allspice and peppercorns in water until all the water has been absorbed. Add oil and sauté until onions are golden. Add garlic and stir-fry for 30 seconds. Add mutton, close saucepan with a tightly-fitting lid and simmer over low heat until meat is well browned and almost done.

Add beans and potatoes, close lid and simmer for 20 minutes until vegetables are almost done. Add chilli, salt, pepper and nutmeg and cook for 10 minutes. Garnish with red pepper. Serve with freshly cooked rice and sambals.

2 large onions, chopped
4 cloves and 4 allspice
2 ml (¹/₂ tsp) peppercorns
125 ml (¹/₂ cup) water
90 ml (6 tbsp) vegetable oil
10 ml (2 tsp) crushed garlic
1 kg (2¹/₄ lb) mutton
2 kg (4¹/₂ lb) French style green beans,
6-8 small potatoes, peeled
1 green chilli, chopped
salt and pepper to taste
5 ml (1 tsp) ground nutmeg

WATERBLOMMETJIE BREDIE

Waterblommetjies grow in the dams and vleis of the Cape. Cut off stems and soak flowers overnight in enough salted water to cover. Use canned waterblommetjies only if fresh waterblommetjies are nowhere to be found. Serves 6-8

Place onions, allspice, cloves and water in a saucepan and simmer until water has evaporated. Add oil and braise until onions are golden. Add meat and garlic and continue braising over low heat until meat is tender and brown and a thick gravy is formed. Drain waterblommetjies; add with potatoes, sorrel and salt.

Close saucepan with tightly-fitting lid and simmer bredie until potatoes are cooked. Sprinkle with freshly ground pepper and serve on a bed of freshly-cooked rice.

3 medium onions, sliced
4 allspice and 2 cloves
2 cloves garlic, finely chopped
125 ml (¹/₂ cup) water
50 ml (4 tbsp) oil
750 g (28 oz) mutton, cubed
1,5 kg (3 lb) waterblommetjies
4 medium potatoes, peeled
and cubed
1 large bunch sorrel
or juice of 2 lemons
5 ml (1 tsp) salt
freshly ground black pepper

KOOLFRIKKADELLE

Koolfrikkadelle are a Cape Malay version of the traditional Turkish dolmas. Substitute vine leaves for cabbage, if available, and prepare in the same way. Serves 8

Place sliced onions, soup bones, allspice, cloves, peppercorns and 250 ml (1 cup) water in a saucepan. Simmer gently.

Mix mince, egg, parsley, mixed herbs, butter, salt and pepper to taste, chopped onion and garlic in a large bowl and set aside.

Separate cabbage leaves and steam for 5 minutes. Wash leaves under cold running water and drain.

Soak sago in 250 ml (1 cup) water. Form mince mixture into balls about the size of golf balls.

Wrap a cabbage leaf around each mince ball and place into saucepan with soup bones. (Add water if required.) Add soaked sago and season with nutmeg, salt and pepper. Steam for 30 minutes. Remove soup bones. Serve on a bed of freshly-cooked rice.

3 medium onions, sliced
250 g (9 oz) soup bones (shin)
5 whole allspice and 5 cloves
5 ml (1 tsp) peppercorns
250 ml (1 cup) water
500 g (18 oz) beef mince
1 egg
25 ml (2 tbsp) chopped parsley
5 ml (1 tsp) mixed herbs
25 ml (2 tbsp) soft butter
salt and pepper to taste
1 onion, chopped
2 cloves garlic, finely chopped
1 spitskop cabbage
60 ml (¹/₄ cup) sago soaked in water
grated nutmeg, salt and pepper to taste

PUMPKIN AND PEAR BREDIE

2 large onions, chopped
250 ml (1 cup) water
4 cloves and 3 allspice
45 ml (3 tbsp) oil
1 kg (2¼ lb) mutton
4 cloves garlic, crushed
4 sticks cinnamon
5 cm-piece root ginger, crushed
2 kg (4¼ lb) pumpkin, peeled and cubed
30 ml (2 tbsp) brown sugar
45 ml (3 tbsp) butter
1 kg (2¼ lb) dried pears
salt and freshly ground pepper to taste

Use Boerpampoen, (flat white pumpkin) or butternut for bredie – the flesh remains firm when cooked. Serves 8

Place onions, water, cloves and allspice in a large saucepan and bring to the boil. Simmer until all the water has been absorbed. Add oil and sauté until onions are golden. Add mutton, garlic, ginger and cinnamon and braise over medium heat until the meat has a rich brown colour and is almost done. Add pumpkin pieces and stir, making sure that meat and pumpkin are well mixed. Close the saucepan with a tightly-fitting lid and allow bredie to simmer until the pumpkin is soft and mushy. By this time the meat must be falling off the bone. Add pears and simmer for 5 minutes. Add brown sugar, butter and seasoning to taste. Serve with freshly-cooked rice.

SMOORSNOEK WITH PICKALA

1 kg (2¼ lb) pickala
50 ml (4 tbsp) vegetable oil
2 medium onions, sliced
1 green chillie
3 large potatoes, peeled and cubed

Fresh snoek cut into mootjies (portions), then washed and salted with coarse salt and packed into wooden barrels where they are left until needed, is called pickala. Serves 6

Soak pickala in water overnight to freshen. Boil in water until cooked, but not mushy. Debone and flake. Heat oil in a saucepan and add onions, chilli and potatoes. Braise over low heat until onions are half cooked. Add pickala, close with a tightly-fitting lid and simmer until potatoes and fish are cooked. Serve with rice and moskonfyt.

YELLOW RICE WITH RAISINS

Yellow rice is popular served as as a separate dish or with Bobotie (see page 81). Serves 6

Place the rice, cinnamon, cardamom pods, turmeric and water in as saucepan. Add the salt and bring to the boil. Turn down heat and cook until rice is tender.

Pour into a colander and rinse under running water to remove excess turmeric. Return to saucepan, add raisins, butter and sugar and steam over low heat until warmed through.

Serve with Plaatfrikkadelle or Bobotie.

500 ml (2 cups) rice
2 sticks cinnamon
3 cardamom pods
2 ml (1/2 tsp) turmeric
1 litre (4 cups) water
salt to taste
250 ml (1 cup) seedless raisins
30 g (1 oz) butter and sugar to taste

SAMP AND BEANS

The amaXhosa people of South Africa traditionally cook samp and beans also lovingly called "diamonds and pearls". Boiled with beef shin, it makes a delightful soup for cold winters. Because it is fairly bland, in Cape Malay cuisine masala is used for flavour. Serves 6

Soak samp and beans in water overnight. Drain and place in a large saucepan. Cover with water, add stock cubes and bring to the boil. Add more water if required. Boil for about 15 minutes over medium heat until water is completely absorbed. Taste to ensure that samp and beans are tender. Remove from heat, add salt, pepper and butter, mix through; keep warm. Sauté onions, potatoes, masala and garlic in oil in saucepan. Add a little water each time until the potatoes are soft. Add potato and onion mixture to the samp and beans and mix through.

500 g (18 oz) samp and bean mix
3 litres (12 cups) water
2 chicken stock cubes
60 ml (4 tbsp) butter
30 ml (2 tbsp) vegetable oil
5 ml (1 tsp) masala
1 medium onion, chopped
2 medium potatoes, peeled and cubed
5 ml (1 tsp) garlic
500 ml (1 cup) water

MAKING A GOOD BREDIE

To make a good bredie a cook's skill is truly put to the test, especially in finding the narrow margin between perfection and over-cooking. Following these tips will go a long way towards cooking a perfect bredie:

- Mutton rib cut into 2 cm/1 inch-cubes is the best meat to use.
- Always braise the meat with onions and spices before adding the vegetables.
- Vegetables are always sliced or chopped and added raw (except in a few cases, for example when you use cabbage).
- Never boil meat in stock or water – this tends to dry out and toughen the meat.
- Don't add liquid. The juices from the vegetables will make a lovely thick gravy.

- Always keep the cooking temperature constant – medium heat – allowing the bredie to simmer gently for a few hours.
- Bredies are best served with rice.

The general technique for making a bredie remains the same, regardless of the specific ingredients. By using different spices, however, completely different flavours are created. Bredies always taste better the day after they are made, or when cooked over an open fire in a heavy-based pot.

(*Potjiekos*, which is currently so popular in South Africa, is nothing more than bredie cooked over an open fire, so *potjiekos* enthusiasts will also benefit from these tips for a perfect bredie!)

DISTRICT SIX POURING BLATJANG

3 dried red chillies
10 cloves garlic
5 ml (1 tsp) ground cumin
5 ml (1 tsp) salt
500 ml (2 cups) smooth apricot jam
enough brown vinegar to give pouring
consistency

Quick to make and ideal for pouring over snoek or frikkadels.

Pound together chillies and garlic until smooth. Stir in cumin and salt. Add apricot jam and blend well.

Whisk in vinegar, a little at a time, tasting occasionally, until you have a balanced sweet-sour flavour and pouring consistency. Add more jam to adjust if the blatjang is too sour.

FISH BOBOTIE

1 kg (2¼ lb) hake, boned and filleted
1 onion, chopped and sautéd in butter
10 ml garlic & ginger paste
10 ml (2 tsp) masala
5 ml(1 tsp) each turmeric & mixed herbs
salt and pepper to taste
25 ml (2 tbsp) lemon juice
50 ml (4 tbsp) brown sugar
100 ml (8 tbsp) chopped parsley
a pinch of nutmeg
6 slices of white bread soaked in milk
300 ml (1¼ cups) milk
2 eggs, beaten with a pinch of salt
4 lemon leaves
100 g (4 oz) flaked almonds

Bobotie does not have to be made with mince to be utterly delicious! You can also use cooked fish instead of raw – just remember to adjust the cooking time. Serves 6

Mince raw fish in a food processor. If you use cooked fish, flake and mince in a food processor. Add chopped, sautéd onion, garlic and ginger paste, masala, turmeric, mixed herbs, salt and pepper, lemon juice, brown sugar, parsley and nutmeg. Squeeze milk from bread and add. Mix well and place in a greased oven-proof dish. Smooth over the top.

Mix all the ingredients for the topping (milk and eggs) except lemon leaves and almonds. Roll lemon leaves into tubes, bruising them slightly to bring out their flavour, and insert into the fish mixture.

Sprinkle with almonds and pour topping over. Bake at 180°C/350°F for 30-40 minutes or until well browned.

Serve with freshly-cooked rice and blatjang.

DHAL CURRY

The Indian influence in Cape Malay cooking is evident in this delicious vegetarian dish. Use brown lentils if oil lentils are not available. Serves 6

375 ml (1½ cups) oil lentils • 2 large onions, chopped • 2 sticks cassia 2 cardamom pods • 60 ml (¼ cup) vegetable oil • 2 medium tomatoes, chopped • 1 green chilli, finely chopped • 10 ml (2 tsp) crushed garlic 15 ml (1 tsp) masala • 5 ml (1 tsp) ground cumin • 5 ml (1 tsp) ground coriander • 2 ml (½ tsp) turmeric • 500 ml (2 cups) water • salt to taste • 3 gem squash • 60 ml (¼ cup) coriander leaves, chopped

Remove grit from lentils; soak in water for 1 hour. Place onions, cassia, cardamom and oil in a saucepan and fry until onions are soft. Add tomatoes, chilli and rest of spices; simmer for 10 minutes. Add drained lentils with 500 ml (2 cups) clean water and salt; simmer over low heat until soft and mushy. Add more water if necessary. Peal gem squashes, cut into rings and remove pips. Layer squash rings over lentil mixture. Close with a tightly fitting lid; simmer until squash rings are tender. Sprinkle with coriander leaves and serve on a bed of rice.

VEGETABLE CURRY

Serve as a filling in rolled roti (see page 50). Serves 6

30 ml (2 tbsp) vegetable oil • 1 large onion, chopped • 1 stick cassia
5 ml (1 tsp) cumin seeds • 2 cardamom pods • 1 large tomato, chopped
1 kg (2¼ lb) mixed vegetables, peeled and chopped • 5 ml (1 tsp)
ginger & garlic paste • 2 ml (½ tsp) turmeric • 5 ml (1 tsp) ground
cumin 5 ml (1 tsp) ground coriander • 5 ml (1 tsp) masala • salt to taste

Heat oil in a large saucepan and fry onion, cumin, cassia and cardamom pods until onions are soft. Add tomatoes and the rest of the
ingredients and stir well. Braise until the vegetables are cooked but not
mushy. Serve with roti and blatjang or a selection of sambals.

PICKLED FISH

1 kg (2¼ lb) snoek cut into portions
2 large onions, sliced
5 cloves garlic, chopped
250 ml (1 cup) vinegar
125 ml (½ cup) water
10 ml (2 tsp) ground coriander
10 ml (2 tsp) ground cumin
15 ml (1 tbsp) masala
5 ml (1 tsp) turmeric
2 bay leaves, 4 allspice & 4 cloves
2 ml (¼ tsp) peppercorns
sugar to taste

A delightful, fragrant dish of curried fish layered with cooked onions and saturated with a sweet-sour sauce. Serves 6-8

Salt fish and fry in vegetable oil until cooked. Remove with a slotted spoon and set aside in a separate bowl; retain oil.

Place the rest of the ingredients except sugar in a saucepan and bring to the boil. Turn down heat and simmer until onions are transparent but haven't lost their crunch.

Add sugar to taste and stir to dissolve. Pour warm sauce and oil over fish, making sure that each portion of fish is covered. Allow to cool and store in a cool place.

Serve with fresh bread and butter.

FRIED SNOEK ROES

500 g (18 oz) snoek roes
a pinch cayenne pepper
a pinch black pepper
salt to taste
1 egg, beaten
vegetable oil for frying
fresh coriander leaves for garnishing

A delightful afternoon snack, snoek roes may also be braised with onions and tomatoes. Serves 4

Wash roes and boil in a little salted water until firm. Drain, set aside and allow to cool. Cut cooked roes into neat portions and season with pepper and salt.

Dip portions into egg end fry in oil until golden brown. Garnish with coriander leaves and serve with wholewheat bread and blatjang.

STAPPIES (SMOORTJIES)

2 medium onions, chopped
15 ml (1 tbsp) vegetable oil
5 cloves garlic & 1 green chilli
2 large tomatoes, chopped
5 ml (1 tsp) each masala, ground cumin, ground coriander
2 ml (½ tsp) turmeric
3 small cans sardines in oil, drained
6 boiled eggs, halved lengthwise
25 ml (2 tbsp) chopped fresh coriander leaves

When unexpected visitors arrive and the hostess realizes that there is not enough food to serve everyone, she will quickly prepare a stappie or smoortjie. *Serves 6*

FAST FISH CURRY

Sauté onions in oil until soft. Pound garlic and chilli to a paste and add to onions. Add tomatoes and spices and mix well. Simmer over low heat for 10 minutes until a thick gravy forms. Carefully add sardines and egg halves and cover with curry sauce. Heat through. Sprinkle with coriander leaves and serve on a bed of freshly-cooked rice.

1 large onion, sliced
10 ml (2 tsp) salt
1 tomato, cubed
60 ml (¼ cup) vinegar
5 ml (1 tsp) sugar
1 can (410 g/14 oz) pilchards
4 hardboiled eggs, halved lengthwise
freshly ground black pepper

SALMON SLAAI

Place onion in bowl; sprinkle with salt. Rub salt into onion with fingertips, squeezing gently until onion is transparent. Place onion in sieve; rinse under cold water to remove juices and salt. Mix with tomato, vinegar and sugar. Add fish, toss. Place in a salad bowl and arrange egg halves on top. Sprinkle with freshly ground black pepper. Serve with bread and butter.

(This fish salad was prepared with canned salmon when it was still relatively inexpensive. Today made with pilchards, it is still known as *Salmon slaai*) in the Cape Malay community.

Mealie bread

Lovely to make when green mealies (corn) are in season. Serves 6

Place the corn kernels in a food processor and process until roughly chopped, or grind with a mincer. Add the rest of the ingredients and mix well. Grease a boston bread mould with butter. Fill 2/3 of the tin with batter and seal tightly with a greased lid. Steam for 2 hours in boiling water. Remove from pan and slice.

Serve with bredies and curries, or grilled snoek.

750 ml (3 cups) mealie kernels, cut from the cob (defrosted corn kernels may also be used)
37,5 ml (3 tbsp) flour
8 ml (1½ tsp) baking powder
25 ml (2 tbsp) butter
12,5 ml (1 tbsp) sugar
5 ml (1 tsp) salt

Braai snoek

Snoek is prepared in many ways, one of the most popular of which is grilling it over hot coals. Serves 6

Season snoek. Place on braai grid, skin side up. Baste regularly with District Six pouring blatjang (*see* page 22). Place apricots on grid and roast until slightly browned. Place apricots on snoek and continue basting. Grill for 20 minutes. Serve immediately with fresh green salad and mealie bread.

1 large splayed snoek (kabeljou or yellowtail)
salt and pepper
District Six pouring blatjang
250 g (8 oz) sundried apricots, soaked in water for 1 hour then drained

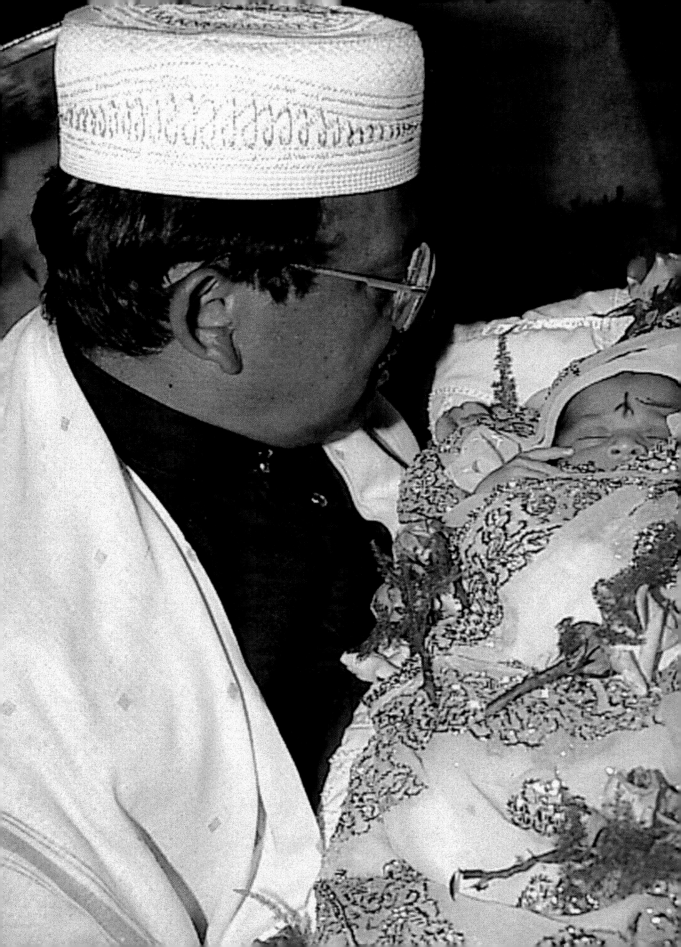

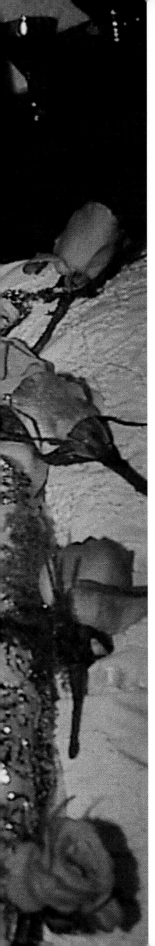

DOOPMAAL

Immediately after the birth of a baby, the father picks up the child and, facing Mecca, intones the call to prayer in the infant's ear. This officially proclaims the child a follower of Islam. On the seventh day after the birth the naming of the child takes place and the occasion calls for a feast – the *doopmaal*. Friends, relatives and an *Imam*, a Muslim priest, attend this celebration.

If the family can afford it, an unblemished sheep is purchased to be sacrificed to Allah (God) to ask that the child be protected from harm, like the son of the prophet Ebrahiem (Abraham) (AS) of old. This sacrifice is called an *Aqiqa*. The meat of the sheep may be enjoyed by the guests present at the doopmaal, or a third may be kept by the family while they distribute two thirds among the needy in the community.

The naming ceremony is simple and takes place in the home of the infant's parents. A special brass tray covered with a beautifully embroidered cushion is used for the ceremony. The baby is dressed in an elaborately hand-embroidered robe and wrapped in a *medora*, a scarf embroidered with solid gold thread. (These scarves are worn by pilgrims on their return from Mecca.)

A dark mark in the shape of a chicken claw is drawn on the infant's forehead with a kohl pencil to keep away the evil eye. Finally rosebuds are arranged around the baby on the tray. The rose is a symbol of the Prophet Mohammed (PBUH). Now the tray is carried to the *Imam* who proceeds with the naming ceremony, normally attended by the men only. During the ceremony a lock of hair is clipped from the baby's head, which symbolises the shaving of babies' hair in olden times. A date or sugar is held to the baby's lips to ensure sweetness in his or her life. After the prayers the tray with the baby is passed around and each man takes a rosebud and pins it to his lapel.

The sumptuousness of the *doopmaal* depends on the means of the baby's parents. Traditionally biscuits and cakes are served. Hot dishes such as Sosaties, Bobotie, Masala Chicken and Fried Vermicelli may also be served, as well as Roast Leg of Lamb from the *aqiqa*.

The only cake recipe in this section which truly originates from the East, is *Kolwadjib*, an unbaked rice cake. Most of the other cake, tart and biscuit recipes have been taken over by the Malay slaves of old from their Dutch masters but soon formed an integral part of their own cuisine.

Milk tart

An all-round favourite with a slightly sweetened short-crust pastry.

750 ml (3 cups) flour
salt to taste
10 ml (2 tsp) baking powder
30 g (1 oz) butter
45 ml (3 tbsp) sugar
2 eggs
a little ice water

PASTRY

Sift flour, salt and baking powder. Cream butter and sugar in a separate bowl. Beat eggs and add to creamed butter and sugar; beat thoroughly. Sift flour into egg mixture and gently mix to form a soft dough. Add a little ice water if necessary. Roll out into 5 mm (¼ inch) thickness and line a loose-bottomed tin of 25 cm (10 inch) diameter. Press dough lightly into tin, neatly finish off edges and prick with fork and brush with lightly beaten egg-white to prevent the dough from becoming soggy.

500 ml (2 cups) sugar
50 ml (4 tbsp) flour
pinch of salt
1 litre (4 cups) milk
5 ml (1 tsp) vanilla essence
4 cardamom pods
2 sticks cinnamon
9 eggs, separated
30 g (1 oz) butter
30 ml (2 tbsp) cinnamon sugar

FILLING

Mix half the sugar with flour and salt. Bring milk to the boil over low heat. Carefully stir the flour mixture into the milk and continue stirring over low heat until the mixture thickens. Remove from heat and add vanilla essence, cardamom and cinnamon. Beat egg yolks. Add the rest of the sugar and beat until mixture is light and creamy. Stir egg mixture into milk mixture. Leave to cool slightly and remove cardamon pods and cinnamon sticks. Beat egg-whites until stiff and fold into filling. Spoon filling into unbaked crust. Dot with butter and sprinkle with cinnamon sugar. Bake at 180°C/350°F for 30 minutes. Reduce heat 160°C/325°F and bake until crust is golden.

Kolwadjib

A sweet, unbaked rice cake of Eastern origin. Decorate with cherries and mint leaves for a festive appearance.

500 ml (2 cups) rice
1,5 litres (6 cups) water
salt to taste
5 ml (1 tsp) pounded naartjie peel or rosewater to taste
5 ml (1 tsp) ground cardamom seed
125 g (4 oz) butter
250 ml (1 cup) brown sugar
250 ml (1 cup) desiccated coconut
glacé cherries and mint leaves for garnishing

Place the rice, water and salt in a large saucepan and bring to the boil. Add naartjie peel or rosewater and cardamom and boil to a thick, mushy consistency.

Add the butter, sugar and coconut and stir over low heat until the sugar has dissolved. Remove from heat and spoon the mixture into a greased tin.

Press down and smooth with the back of a spoon. Leave to cool. Cut into neat squares and decorate with cherries and mint leaves.

Ginger beer

Traditionally served in summer. Makes 5 litres

5 litres (20 cups) boiling water
240 g (8 oz) sugar
30 ml (2 tbsp) ground ginger
10 ml (2 tsp) active dry yeast
15 ml (3 tsp) tartaric acid
15 ml (3 tsp) cream of tartar
250 ml (1 cup) raisins

Pour boiling water into a large saucepan. Add sugar. Stir until sugar dissolves then add ginger. Simmer for about 30 minutes. Leave to cool. When lukewarm add all remaining ingredients.

Cover and keep in a warm place for 2 days to mature. Chill and serve in tall glasses (illustrated on page 30).

GESKROEIDE VERMICELLI

*This popular pudding with toasted vermicelli or lokshen is served
at most feasts, including* Tamat, Eid-ul-Fitr *and weddings.*
Serves 6

Melt butter in a saucepan; add cinnamon and cardamom pods. Break
vermicelli into smaller pieces or lightly crush lokshen and toast in butter until light-brown.

Add water little by little, cooking lokshen or vermicelli until soft and
all the water has been absorbed.

Add sugar, carefully stirring until dissolved. Fork in sultanas and
almonds, working carefully not to mash lokshen or vermicelli. Serve on
side-plates.

250 g (9 oz) butter
3 sticks cinnamon
4 cardamom pods
250 g (9 oz) vermicelli
or 1 packet lokshen
500 ml (2 cups) water
sugar to taste
125 ml (½ cup) sultanas
100 g (4 oz) flaked almonds

SPICY ICED HONEYBUSH TEA

500 ml (2 cups) Honeybush tea
1 stick cinnamon
4 cloves
pinch of nutmeg
1,5 litres (6 cups) ginger ale
fresh mint leaves to garnish

Since no alcohol is ever served at any traditional Cape Malay celebrations, a lot of time and effort will go into preparing interesting beverages such as this iced tea. Makes 2 litres

Boil honeybush tea with cinnamon, cloves and nutmeg for 10 minutes. Strain, allow to cool. Add ginger ale and mint, then chill. Serve cold with ice and mint leaves.

FRUIT REFRESHER

500 ml (2 cups) Rooibos tea, chilled
250 ml (1 cup) orange juice
250 ml (1 cup) pineapple juice
orange slices to garnish

Use strong tea and add granadilla pulp, banana slices, maraschino cherries or strawberries to make this drink it more interesting and to add additional flavour. Makes 1 litre

Mix together all ingredients except the orange slices. Chill thoroughly. Serve garnished with orange slices.

Sambouras

Crisp biscuits traditionally decorated with currants. Makes 48

Cream sugar and butter or dripping well in a large mixing bowl. Add oil and beat until creamy. Add spices and flavouring; mix to blend. Beat eggs thoroughly, add to creamed mixture and beat well. Sift flour, baking powder and salt together. Add to egg mixture and mix to form a stiff dough that can be rolled out. Roll out to 5 mm (¼ inch) thickness. Cut out oblong shapes with biscuit cutter. Sprinkle with sugar and press 3 currants into each shape, one at the top, one in the middle and one at the bottom (Sambouras are traditionally decorated like this). Place on a greased baking sheet and bake for 20 minutes at 180°C/350°F. Carefully loosen biscuits and cool on a wire rack.

310 ml (1¼ cups) yellow sugar
60 g (2 oz) butter or dripping
80 ml (⅓ cup) vegetable oil
2 ml (½ tsp) ground cardamom
5 ml (1 tsp) ground ginger
5 ml (1 tsp) rosewater
2 eggs
4 x 250 ml (4 cups) flour
10 ml (2 tsp) baking powder
pinch of salt
currants and sugar for garnishing

Coconut scraps

For variation, sprinkle sugar over biscuits before baking.
Makes 60

Sift flour and salt. Rub in butter until mixture resembles breadcrumbs. Beat eggs and vanilla essence. Add sugar a little at a time and beat until sugar is dissolved. Add coconut to flour and mix. Add this to egg mixture and mix to a dough that can be rolled out. Add a little oil if the dough is too stiff.

Roll out to 10 mm (½ inch) thickness. Cut into shapes with a biscuit cutter, sprinkle with sugar and place a halved cherry in the centre of each biscuit.

Place on a greased baking sheet and bake at 180°C/350°F until golden. Loosen biscuits and cool on a wire rack. These biscuits should be stored in an airtight container to retain crispness.

4 x 250 ml (4 cups) flour
salt to taste
150 g (5 oz) butter
2 eggs
5 ml (1 tsp) vanilla essence
250 ml (1 cup) sugar
250 ml (1 cup) desiccated coconut
a little vegetable oil
halved glacé cherries and sugar
for garnishing

Rulle

Always popular at both the doopmaal *and engagement celebrations. Making these deep-fried delicacies is hard work but well worth the effort. Makes 60*

Cream sugar, butter and dripping or margarine until light and fluffy. Add beaten eggs and mix until smooth.

Sift flour, baking powder, salt, spices and naartjie peel. Mix milk, kaiings and bicarbonate of soda.

Add milk mixture and flour mixture alternately to egg mixture to make a stiff dough that can be rolled out. Mix well to get rid of any lumps. Add more flour if necessary.

Roll out dough to 10 mm (½ inch) thickness. Cut into diamond shapes. Deep-fry until golden brown. Lift out with slotted spoon and drain on paper towel.

Sprinkle with cinnamon sugar while rulle are still warm.

625 ml (2½ cups) sugar
60 g (2 oz) butter
250 8 (8 oz) dripping/margarine
2 eggs, beaten
4 x 250 ml (4 cups) flour
10 ml (2 tsp) baking powder
pinch of salt
10 ml (2 tsp) each pounded naartjie peel
and ground cinnamon, cardamom and
ginger
250 ml (1 cup) kaiings(brownsels)
2 ml (½ tsp) bicarbonate of soda
milk to mix
vegetable oil for frying
cinnamon sugar

Coconut tartlets

The secret of successful flaky pastry is to keep it cool and bake it in a hot oven. Makes 24

EASY FLAKY PASTRY

750 ml (3 cups) cake flour
5 ml (1 tsp) baking powder
a pinch of salt
500 g (10 oz) butter
15 ml (1 tbsp) vinegar
325 ml (1½ cups) ice water

Sift together flour, baking powder and salt. Grate in the butter and mix. Add vinegar to water and mix into flour mixture. Lightly form dough into a ball and refrigerate for 2 hours. Turn out onto floured surface and roll out into rectangle about 10 mm (½ inch) thick. Fold dough in half from short side to short side; fold in half again in same direction; fold in half from left to right to form square. Place in refrigerator for 1 hour. Roll and fold as above three more times before using. Remove from refrigerator before required.

FILLING

250 ml (1 cup) sugar
500 ml (2 cups) desiccated coconut
125 ml (½ cup) water
5 ml vanilla essence

Place all ingredients in a saucepan and bring to the boil over low heat. Cook, stirring all the time, until filling has a smooth, soft consistency. Avoid overcooking which makes it tough and sticky. Roll out pastry to 5 mm (¼ inch) thickness, cut into rounds and place in patty pans. Place 15 ml (1 tbsp) filling in centre of each round and cover with strips of left-over dough. Brush pastry with beaten egg yolk. Bake at 200°C/400°F until a rich golden colour.

Essies

Crisp, sweet biscuits with a lovely combination of spices baked in interestingly coloured S-shapes, hence the name Essies. Makes 84

750 ml (3 cups) flour
5 ml (1 tsp) each salt, bicarbonate of soda
5 ml (1 tsp) cream of tartar
5 ml (1 tsp) ground nutmeg
5 ml (1 tsp) each ground cloves and ground cinnamon
5 ml (1 tsp) ground ginger
375 ml (1½ cups) brown sugar
125 g (4 oz) butter
50 g (2 oz) fat
3 eggs
5 ml (1 tsp) red bole

Sift flour, salt, bicarbonate of soda, cream of tartar and spices. Add sugar and mix. Rub butter and fat into flour mixture with fingertips. Beat eggs, add to flour mixture and form a dough that can be rolled out. Divide the dough into two rough chunks of equal size. Mix red bole (food colouring obtainable from pharmacies) into one chunk.

Roll dough into small balls. Press each red ball into a white ball, roll into a snake and form an 'S'. Place on a greased baking sheet and bake at 180°C/350°F for 10-12 minutes.

Loosen biscuits and cool on wire rack.

Butter biscuits

Place the dough in the refrigerator if it becomes too soft. Makes 96

4 x 250 ml (4 cups) flour
10 ml (2 tsp) baking powder
salt to taste
300 ml (1¼ cups) sugar
250 g (½ lb) butter
2 eggs
glacé cherries and watermelon preserve for garnishing

Sift flour, baking powder and salt. Add sugar and mix. Rub butter into flour and sugar. Beat eggs, add to flour mixture and mix to form dough without handling it too much. Roll out on floured surface and cut into shapes with a biscuit cutter. Decorate each biscuit with a piece of cherry and preserve. Place on a greased baking sheet and bake at 180°C/350°F for 12-15 minutes. Loosen biscuits and cool on wire rack.

KARAMONK SCRAPS

These delicacies are crisp cardamom biscuits. Makes 72

Cream butter and sugar. Add oil or dripping and mix well. Beat eggs separately, then beat into creamed mixture. Sift flour and baking powder; add coconut, cardamom and naartjie peel. Add dry ingredients to creamed mixture and mix to a dough that can be rolled out. Roll out on floured surface to 5 mm (1/4 inch) thickness. Print a pattern on the dough with the tines of a fork and cut into squares. Decorate with a walnut in the centre of each square. Place on a greased baking sheet and bake at 180°C/350°F for 15-20 minutes. Loosen biscuits and cool on wire rack.

250 g (9 oz) butter
625 ml (2 1/2 cups) sugar
60 ml (1/4 cup) vegetable oil or dripping
2 eggs
8 x 250 ml (8 cups) flour
10 ml (2 tsp) baking powder
375 ml (1 1/2 cups) desiccated coconut
7 cardamom pods, finely pounded
5 ml (1 tsp) finely-pounded
naartjie peel
walnuts for garnishing

RAISIN TART

A sweet open tart, delicious served with whipped cream.

PASTRY
Prepare flaky pastry according to recipe on page 32.

FILLING
Place raisins, sultanas and water in a saucepan and simmer until raisins and sultanas are plump. Add sugar, butter and cinnamon. Simmer until mixture is almost dry. The filling should not be watery. Roll out pastry to 5 mm (1/2 inch) thickness. Line a 25 cm (10 inch) pie dish with pastry. Cut left-over pastry into long strips 10 mm (1/2 inch) wide. Spoon filling into pie dish and place strips of pastry in a criss-cross pattern over the filling. Brush pastry with beaten egg yolk. Bake at 200°C/400°F for 30 minutes. Allow to cool and serve with whipped cream.

250 ml (1 cup) seedless raisins
250 ml (1 cup) sultanas
250 ml (1 cup) water
80 ml (1/3 cup) sugar
15 ml (1 tbsp) butter
ground cinnamon to taste

KORENTEKOLWYNTJIES

Sweet muffins with currants, traditionally decorated with brightly-coloured icing, although I prefer to serve them just with a dusting of icing sugar. Makes 24

4 x 250 ml (4 cups) self-raising flour • salt to taste • 125 g (4 oz) butter • 200 ml (3/4 cup) sugar • 2 eggs • 375 ml (1 1/2 cups) milk 5 ml (1 tsp) vanilla essence • 250 ml (1 cup) currants • icing sugar for garnishing

Sift flour and salt. Cream butter and sugar until light and fluffy. Beat eggs; add to creamed mixture and beat well. Sift flour into creamed mixture and mix to form a soft but not runny batter. Add milk if too stiff. Add vanilla essence and currants and mix.

Spoon into greased muffin pans and bake at 180°C/350°F for 20-25 minutes. Loosen edges; allow to cool before turning out. Dust with sifted icing sugar.

Baby wrapped in gold-embroidered medora with rosebuds strewn around

CHICKEN KEBABS

6 chicken breasts
12-15 bamboo skewers
5 ml (1 tsp) vegetable oil
10 ml (2 tsp) crushed garlic
5 ml (1 tsp) masala
5 ml (1 tsp) ground cumin
5 ml (1 tsp) crushed root ginger
2 ml (½ tsp) turmeric
2 ml (½ tsp) ground coriander
salt to taste
oil to baste or fry kebabs
peanut & tamarind blatjang

An old Eastern tradition using strips of chicken fried or grilled on bamboo skewers, served with and interesting chutney, such as peanut and tamarind blatjang, as a dipping sauce. Serves 6

Cut chicken breasts into strips of 1 x 5 cm/½ x 2 inches. Folding them over, thread the strips of chicken onto the bamboo skewers. Mix oil, garlic, masala, cumin, ginger, coriander and salt into a paste and rub over the kebabs.

Leave to to marinate for at least one hour.

Grill or fry the kebabs in oil for 3 minutes. When grilling, baste the kebabs regularly. Garnish with fresh coriander leaves and serve with peanut and tamarind blatjang.

Roast leg of lamb

The leg of lamb is obtained from the sheep used for the Aqiqa.
Serves 6

1,5 kg (3½ lb) leg of lamb • 5 garlic cloves • 6 cloves • salt and freshly-ground pepper to taste • 90 ml (⅓ cup) vegetable oil • 2 bay leaves • 6 medium potatoes, peeled and halved • 6 baby marrows, cleaned, trimmed and halved

Spike leg of lamb and press garlic cloves and cloves into holes. Season liberally with salt and pepper. Pour oil into a roasting pan, add leg of lamb and tuck bay leaves under the meat.

Roast at 200°C/400°F for 15 minutes on each side, turning once, to seal the meat. Turn down heat to 180°C/ 350°F and roast for 1½ hours until meat is just done.

Place potatoes around meat and roast for 30-40 minutes. Add baby marrows 10 minutes before meat is done. Serve with Sousboontjies.

Masala fish

Fresh fish marinated in an exceptionally aromatic mixture of spices.
Serves 6-8

Pound together cumin seeds, coriander seeds, garlic, chillies and salt (if a food processor or blender is used, add garlic cloves while the blade is running to prevent cloves from getting stuck under the blades). Add turmeric and masala to form a thick paste.

Rub paste into fish portions and leave to marinate for 15 minutes. Heat oil and fry fish for 8-10 minutes on each side until cooked. Be careful not to overcook. Remove from pan, arrange on a serving platter and sprinkle with lemon juice.

Fry tomato slices in same oil for 2 minutes and layer on top op fish. Serve with roti and sambals.

30 ml (2 tbsp) cumin seeds
30 ml (2 tbsp) coriander seeds
10 cloves garlic
2 green chillies
10 ml (2 tsp) salt
5 ml (1 tsp) turmeric
15 ml (1 tbsp) masala
1 kg (2/ lb) snoek or firm-fleshed fish, cut into portions
vegetable oil for frying
juice of 3 lemons
3 medium tomatoes cut into thick slices

Sousboontjies

Quick and easy to prepare if you use canned sugar beans. If dried beans are used, soak in water overnight and boil until soft but not mushy. Serves 6

Place onions, vinegar, garlic, chilli, brown sugar, cloves, allspice, peppercorns and bay leaf into a saucepan. Bring to the boil and simmer for 15 minutes over low heat.

Taste and adjust sugar/vinegar quantities if necessary to obtain a good sweet-sour balance.

Add beans in their juice and continue simmering for 15 minutes. Season to taste and allow to cool. Serve with roast leg of lamb or plaatfrikkadelle.

1 onion, chopped
250 ml (1 cup) brown vinegar
10 ml (2 tsp) crushed garlic
1 green chilli, finely chopped
60-90 ml (¼ -⅓ cup) brown sugar
2 cloves
4 allspice
2 ml (½ tsp) peppercorns
1 bay leaf
2 cans (410 g/14 oz each) sugar beans
salt and pepper to taste

TAMAT

The *Madressa* or Muslim religious school is one of the main vehicles for the teaching of religion and culture. All Muslim children from the age of about six attend these schools in the afternoon after their regular (secular) lessons, usually for the full duration of their primary school career. At the *Madressa* they receive tuition in elementary religious teachings as well as the reading of the Koran, which is written in Arabic. The *Madressa* plays a very important role in preserving the Islamic culture and heritage.

When a child has completed this Islamic education and recited the Koran from cover to cover a colourful ceremony takes place as this is an occasion for rejoicing by the entire community. Boys are dressed in Arabian attire which includes a *sorbaan*, or turban, adorning their heads. Children are are normally accompanied to the mosque by attendants dressed in the same way.

At the mosque they have to read and recite sections from the Koran and are tested on their knowledge of elementary Islamic teachings by *Imams* invited by their parents to do the testing.

This is known as the *Tamat* ceremony, which also signifies a child's entry into adulthood.

After the *Tamat* ceremony all present at the mosque as well as neighbours and friends are invited to join the extended family in celebration at home. Festivities continue as long as the food lasts. The opulence of the feast depends on the means of the child's parents. Usually tea is served with a selection of cakes similar to those served at the *Doopmaal*, followed by a sumptuous warm meal.

Popular warm dishes include Snoek Beryani and *Gesmoorde rys* (braised rice).

Traditional *Tamat* has virtually died out in the Cape Malay community and has been replaced by a children's day at various *Madressas*.

MASALA CHICKEN

1 kg (2¼ lb) chicken pieces
10 ml (2 tsp) masala
5 ml (1 tsp) ground cumin
5 ml (1 tsp) ground coriander
5 ml (1 tsp) turmeric
15 ml (1 tbsp) crushed garlic
15 ml (1 tbsp) crushed ginger
1 green chilli, finely chopped
salt and pepper to taste
30 ml (2 tbsp) vegetable oil
80 ml (⅓ cup) vegetable oil for basting

Although masala can be bought ready to use, try making your own (see page 14) for a special occasions. Dip lemon wedges into a mixture of chilli powder and salt for an attractive garnishing that adds piquancy. Serves 6

Trim chicken pieces. Mix together spices, garlic, ginger, chilli, salt and pepper. Add oil and mix to a paste. Rub paste onto chicken and leave for 1 hour.

Place chicken in a baking tray, baste with oil and roast at 180°C/350°F for 45 minutes or until chicken is cooked.

Serve on a platter with tomato and lemon wedges.

SNOEK BERYANI

4 x 250 ml (4 cups) rice
2 sticks cinnamon
2 cardamom pods
10 ml (2 tsp) salt
2 kg (4 ¼ lb) snoek, cut into portions
125 ml (½ cup) vegetable oil
2 large onions, sliced
5 potatoes, peeled and quartered
2 pinches saffron, soaked in 250 ml
1 cup) boiling water
50 g (2 oz) butter, cubed
MARINADE
1 stick cinnamon
6 cloves & 2 cardamom pods
1 ml (¼ tsp) peppercorns
5 ml (1 tsp) turmeric
10 ml (2 tsp) ground coriander
10 ml (2 tsp) ground cumin
5 ml (1 tsp) ground fennel
6 cloves garlic, crushed
2 tomatoes, skinned and chopped
500 ml (2 cups) natural yoghurt
salt to taste

Although fish is generally regarded as huiskos, more elaborate fish dishes such as this beryani and Gesmoorde snoek (see page 77) are prepared for special occasions. Although saffron is expensive, no beryani is complete without it. Serves 6-8

Place rice in a saucepan with cinnamon, cardamom pods and salt to taste. Add enough water to cover rice. Bring to the boil and boil for 10 minutes. Drain in a colander, rinse with cold water and set aside.

Season fish portions with salt and fry in heated oil for about 3 minutes on each side. Remove from pan and place in a large, flat bowl.

MAKE THE MARINADE: Mix together all ingredients for marinade and pour over fish, making sure that each portion is well coated. Allow to marinate for at least 30 minutes.

COMPLETING THE LAYERS: Fry onions in oil used to fry fish, until soft and golden. Remove with a slotted spoon and set aside. Fry potatoes in same oil until golden brown. Remove and set aside.

Pour remaining oil into a large saucepan. Sprinkle 250 ml (1 cup) rice over oil and arrange fish slices with marinade and half the fried onions on top of the rice.

Layer potatoes over fish and cover with rest of rice. Top with remaining onions. Pour over saffron water and dot with butter.

Close saucepan with a tightly-fitting lid and simmer for 45 minutes over low heat.

Serve with *Dhai* (see page 78).

SAMBALS

Sambals are served with almost every Cape Malay meal – cool sambals with hot dishes, and hot sambals with bland dishes to add interest and piquancy. Sambals must never by allowed to lose their colour and crispness and are best made immediately before serving. The traditional combination is cucumber, tomato and chilli with vinegar and fresh coriander leaves, but any fruit or vegetables can be used.

QUINCE SAMBAL

1 large ripe quince • 60 ml (1/4 cup) lemon juice • 45 ml (3 tbsp) sugar
2 green chillies, finely chopped • salt and pepper to taste

Grate quince into lemon juice. Add all the other ingredients and mix well. Serve immediately with curry and rice or fish.

CUCUMBER SAMBAL

1 English cucumber • 60 ml (4 tbsp) finely chopped fresh coriander leaves • 10 ml (2 tsp) sugar • 1 green chilli, finely chopped • salt to taste • 60 ml (1/4 cup) vinegar or lemon juice

Grate cucumber and drain. Add the rest of the ingredients, mix well and serve with any meat dish.

CARROT SAMBAL

4 medium carrots, grated • 60 ml (4 tbsp) chopped fresh coriander leaves • 60 ml (1/4 cup) orange juice • 1 green chilli, finely chopped salt to taste

Mix all ingredients and serve with any meat dish.

On their way home from the Madressa

PLAATFRIKKADELLE

These meatballs are called 'Plaatfrikkadelle' because they were traditionally baked on a bakplaat or baking sheet. Serves 6

Soak bread in water. Sauté onions in butter until transparent. Add to beef mince in a mixing bowl. Squeeze out water from bread, add to mince with all the other ingredients and mix thoroughly. Form into large meatballs.

Place in a greased ovenproof dish. Bake at 180°C/350°F for 40 minutes or until cooked and brown. Garnish with chopped parsley. Serve with Sweet saffron rice and Date salad (*see* pages 41, 43).

4 thick slices of stale bread
2 onions, finely chopped
30 ml (2 tbsp) butter
1 kg (2 1/4 lb) beef mince
5 ml (1 tsp) dried mixed herbs
6 cloves garlic, finely chopped
2 ml (1/2 tsp) nutmeg
5 ml (1 tsp) salt
freshly ground black pepper
60 ml (4 tbsp) chopped parsley

PIENANG CURRY

*A mild lamb curry simmered until all the flavours have blended to form an aromatic whole which is a true taste sensation.
Serves 6*

Pound bay leaves, cloves, allspice, garlic and cassia into a paste. Heat oil in a saucepan and sauté onions and paste until onions are transparent. Add cubed lamb and cover saucepan with a tightly-fitting lid. Simmer over low heat for 35 minutes.

Mix masala, turmeric, strained tamarind liquid or lemon juice, sugar and salt. Carefully pour over the meat, making sure that each piece of meat is adequately covered. Close lid and simmer for 20 minutes or until meat is tender. Serve with jasmine-flavoured rice.

2 bay leaves
2 whole cloves & 4 allspice
5 fat cloves garlic & 2 sticks cassia
2 large onions, sliced
50 ml (4 tbsp) vegetable oil
1 kg (2 1/4 lb) lamb, cubed
15 ml (1 tbsp) masala
10 ml (2 tsp) turmeric
small piece tamarind soaked in 125 ml (1/2 cup) water or juice of 2 lemons
30 ml (2 tbsp) brown sugar
salt to taste

SABANANGVLEIS

125 g (5 oz) butter
2 large onions, chopped
10 ml (2 tsp) crushed garlic
1 kg (2¼ lb) mutton mince
500 g (18 oz) boiled potatoes, mashed
salt and pepper to taste
10 ml (2 tsp) masala
5 ml (1 tsp) turmeric
80 ml (⅓ cup) Bulgarian yoghurt
4 cloves & 4 bay leaves
60 g (2 oz) butter

An unusual mutton dish with a delicious, mild curry flavour.
Serves 6

Melt 125 g (4 oz) butter in a saucepan and sauté onions and garlic until golden. Add mince and braise, stirring all the time to prevent lumps, until meat is well browned.

Remove from heat; mix in mashed potatoes, salt, pepper, masala, turmeric and yoghurt and spoon into a greased, oven-proof dish. Smooth over surface and press cloves and bay leaves into meat. Dot with butter and bake at 180°C/350°F until heated through and golden brown. Serve with rice.

Rack of lamb with denningvleis sauce

A most attractive meat dish served with one of the oldest and most favoured Cape Malay sauces with an exciting combination of spices. Serves 6

6 lamb racks • salt and pepper to taste

Place seasoned racks in the oven at 210°C/425°F for 20-30 minutes. Remove from oven and keep warm.

DENNINGVLEIS SAUCE
3 large onions, chopped • 25 ml (2 tbsp) vegetable oil • 5 plump cloves of garlic, crushed • 5 allspice • 6 cloves • 2 bay leaves • 1 chilli, finely chopped • 10 ml (2 tsp) freshly ground black pepper • 5 ml (1 tsp) grated nutmegsalt to taste • 25 ml (2 tbsp) seedless tamarind soaked in 250 ml boiling water

Place all ingredients (except tamarind) in a saucepan. Mix the tamarind well with the water and pour into saucepan over the other ingredients. Bring to the boil and simmer until the sauce is thick and shiny. Serve with racks of lamb.

Kabobs

The traditional Cape Malay kabobs are made with boiled eggs. Makes 8-10

6 slices white bread soaked in water
1 kg (2¼ lb) beef mince
1 large onion, very finely chopped
5 ml (1 tsp) crushed garlic
2 eggs, beaten
30 ml (2 tbsp) butter
2 ml (½ tsp) nutmeg
salt and pepper to taste
8-10 hard-boiled eggs, shelled
vegetable oil for frying
1 bay leaf
lemon and tomato for garnishing

Squeeze water out of bread. Place in a bowl; add rest of ingredients except eggs and bay leaf. Mix well. Make a hollow in the mixture.

Place a wood-coal in a metal container in the hollow and cover with a thick cloth or blanket to retain the smoke and give the meat a smoky flavour. Allow to smoke for 40 minutes. Remove coal and cover each egg with mince mixture.

Heat oil with bay leaf; fry kabobs on all sides, continuously basting, until golden brown. Garnish with lemon and tomato wedges and serve with blatjang.

Sweet saffron rice

This is only made for special occasions because saffron is so expensive. Serves 6

500 ml (2 cups) Jasmin-flavoured rice
1,5 litres (6 cups) water
salt to taste
2 sticks cinnamon
4 cardamom pods
2 ml (½ tsp) saffron
125 ml (½ cup) sugar
100 g (4 oz) butter or margarine

Place rice, water, salt, cinnamon and cardamom pods in a large saucepan and bring to the boil. Turn down heat, cover with a tightly-fitting lid and cook until rice is almost done. Drain in a colander and rinse in cold water.

Return to saucepan and add saffron, sugar and butter. Stir gently over low heat and replace lid. Steam for 20 minutes.

MINCE CURRY

60 ml (¹/₄ cup) vegetable oil
2 large onions, finely chopped
2 sticks cassia
4 cardamom pods & 4 cloves
1 sprig curry leaves
1 kg (2¹/₄ lb) beef mince
1 can (410 g/14 oz) chopped tomatoes
10 ml (2 tsp) each ground cumin and
ground coriander
15 ml (1 tbsp) masala
3 ml (¹/₂ tsp) turmeric
30 ml (2 tbsp) garlic and ginger paste
500 g (18 oz) frozen peas
6 boiled eggs, peeled and halved

The addition of peas and boiled eggs gives this otherwise ordinary-looking mince dish a festive appearance. Quick and easy to make, it also serves as a filling for roti, in vetkoek and sandwiches.
Serves 6-8

Heat oil in saucepan and sauté onions, cassia, cardamom, cloves and curry leaves until onions are golden brown. Be careful not to burn the ponions as this leaves a bitter taste.

Add mince and braise until browned. Add tomatoes, cumin, coriander, masala, turmeric and garlic and ginger paste. Close with a tightly-fitting lid and simmer for 30 minutes.

Add frozen peas and simmer until peas are cooked. Add eggs; spoon meat gravy over eggs. Simmer for 5 minutes. Sprinkle with fresh, chopped coriander leaves and serve with rice.

GESMOORDE RYS

Cook braised rice in a saucepan with a tightly-fitting lid to ensure that the flavours are retained. Serves 6-8

1 large onion, chopped • 5 ml (1 tsp) cumin seeds • 3 cardamom pods
2 sticks cassia • 3 each allspice and cloves • 60 ml (¹/₄ cup) vegetable
oil • 500 ml (2 cups) rice • 10 ml (2 tsp) salt • 1 litre (4 cups) water
15 ml (1 tbsp) butter

Sauté onion, cumin seeds, cardamom, cassia, allspice and cloves in oil until onions are soft and golden. Add rice and stir-fry for 2 minutes, then add salt and water. Bring to the boil. Cover with a tightly-fitting lid, turn down the heat and simmer until the rice is cooked and all the water has been absorbed (20-25 minutes). Toss butter into hot rice before serving. This spicy rice enhances the flavour of any curry.

PERLEMOEN FRIKKADELS

Milder seasoning is used for this abalone dish in order to retain its delicate flavour. Serves 6

600 g (22 oz) minced perlemoen (abalone) • 1 small onion, finely
chopped • 2 cloves garlic, crushed • 30 ml (2 tbsp) chilli sauce • 30 ml
(2 tbsp) chopped parsley • 10 ml (2 tsp) freshly ground black pepper
1 large egg, lightly beaten • salt to taste • breadcrumbs for coating
vegetable oil for frying

Mix all the ingredients except breadcrumbs and oil in a bowl. Shape into patties and coat with breadcrumbs. Allow to rest in fridge for 15 minutes. Heat oil and fry patties for 5-8 minutes on each side or until golden brown. Serve on a bed of rice with blatjang.

Young boys at the mosque attending the Tamat ceremony of their older friends

FENUGREEK VEGETABLE CURRY

Do not be tempted to add water to the curry, as the vegetables will release sufficient moisture to create a sauce. Be careful not to overcook the vegetables. They have to be crisp when served. Serves 6

Sauté onions in oil until transparent. Add carrots, all the spices, garlic and ginger and sauté for 2 minutes. Add assorted vegetables (use red and green peppers, cut into thick strips; sliced patty pan marrows, button mushrooms and courgettes, shredded spinach, cauliflower florets and baby corn spears for an attractive mix). Llower heat and stir-fry so that the spices and vegetables are mixed through.

Add potatoes just before serving and stir through. Garnish with fresh coriander leaves.

1 large onion, sliced
70 ml (¹/₃ cup) vegetable oil
100 g (3 oz) carrots, cleaned and sliced
1 pinch fenugreek seeds
5 ml (1 tsp) whole cumin
5 ml (1 tsp) fragrant masala
2,5 ml (¹/₂ tsp) turmeric
10 ml (2 tsp) ground cumin
10 ml (2 tsp) ground coriander
10 ml (2 tsp) garlic & 5 ml (1 tsp) ginger
1 kg (2¹/₄ lb) assorted prepared vegetables
100 g (3 oz) baby potatoes, boiled
salt to taste

DATE SALAD

An unusual salad that enhances the flavour of bredies and curries.

Pour boiling water over onions. Leave for 5 minutes, drain and allow to cool. Layer chopped dates with onions in a glass bowl. Mix chillies, salt, sugar and vinegar and pour over dates and onions. Allow to stand for at least 2 hours for the flavours to develop. Serve with any meat dish.

boiling water
2 large onions, thinly sliced
500 g (18 oz) stoned dates, chopped
5 ml (1 tsp) crushed red chillies
salt and sugar to taste
250 ml (1 cup) brown vinegar

RAMADAN

Fasting during the month of Ramadan is one of the five pillars of Islam and is compulsory for every Muslim over the age of puberty. Pregnant women (if they feel that fasting may harm them or the baby), travellers and women who are menstruating are exempted from the fast, but are obliged to fast at a later stage for the number of days they have missed. Instead of fasting, people who are ill, and old people, have to supply a needy person with food daily, or pay a penalty to the poor in the form of rice or its monetary equivalent.

The fast commences with the sighting of the new moon at the beginning of the ninth month of the Muslim calender and terminates at the sighting of the new moon at the beginning of the tenth month – a period of 29-30 days. During the fast no food, drink or any other substance may enter the body from sunrise to sunset. Smoking is not allowed. Children from the age of six are encouraged to take part in the fast, even if only for half a day. As they get older the time is increased until they are able to fast for the entire day.

Ramadan is particularly trying for women with families who, in addition to performing their normal daily tasks and cooking for the family, have to cook titbits and make sweetmeats to send to their neighbours every evening. A woman's day starts an hour before sunrise when she rises to prepare *Saur* (breakfast) for the family. In view of the long day ahead and out of general concern she will often prepare whatever each individual member of the family desires. Breakfast usually consists of fruit juices, porridge such as oatmeal or mealiemeal, toast and tea or coffee. Men working as builders or in other physically demanding jobs may request chops, eggs or other protein-rich food to help sustain their energy through the day. The family must stop eating before sunrise and the call to prayers.

When the woman returns from work, or after completing her housework, she has to cook the evening meal. She cooks her family's favourite dishes, as well as a pot of traditional soup. Because she is fasting she may not taste the food she cooks. Besides the evening meal she makes something special to send to her neighbours. These sweetmeats or savoury titbits vary from day to day, so one can imagine what creativity she has to display to come up with something new and exciting every day. This chapter is dedicated to all the wonderful Muslim women who often ask me for recipes to prepare these delicacies.

At sunset the family gather around the table which is beautifully laid with dates, water and a variety of delicacies received from the neighbours. There may be more than ten different varieties of titbits on the

Well-wishing after Eid prayers

table at any one time. At the call to evening prayers the fast is broken. Traditionally, after a short prayer, each person will have a date and a sip of water. This is followed by soup and, since the body craves sweet and oily foods as a result of the fast, the sweetmeats and savoury titbits are eaten next. The main meal follows after the evening prayers. Many families have their main meal when they return from the mosque prayers which take place every night during the fast.

The fast of Ramadan is often likened to climbing a mountain. The first 14 days are uphill and difficult as the body adjusts to the lack of food. As the fast progresses the stomach shrinks and less food is consumed. When the peak is reached on the 15th day a large pot of boeber (similar to *melkkos*) is made and sent out to the neighbours to celebrate. Many a non-Muslim neighbour also waits impatiently for the *boeber* sent out on the 15th day!

The final days of the fast are much easier and are also occupied by everyone in the household painting and cleaning the house in preparation for the 27th night, 'The Night of Power', when the Koran was revealed to the faithful. This is also the night when forgiveness of sin is granted. 'The Night of Power' has also been called *kers opsteek*, because when electricity was unavailable many candles were lit in each room of the house to symbolise the light which descended on humanity with the revelation of the Koran. In many households candles are still lit, despite the availability of electric lighting.

A few days before the sighting of the new moon Muslim households are abustle with preparations for *Eid-ul-Fitr (Labarang Ramadan)*. New clothes are bought for all the members of the family and the womenfolk start baking cakes and biscuits and planning the menu for the feast which terminates the fast.

At the end of Ramadan men from the community gather at Green Point and Camps Bay for the sighting of the new moon and Muslims all over the Peninsula are informed as soon as it is sighted.

Now Beryani, which has to be marinated overnight, and as much as possible of the food for the feast that can be made beforehand, are prepared. This leaves the women free to entertain the many guests who will arrive the next day to wish the family well.

On the morning of *Eid-ul-Fitr* the men attend the *Eid* prayers at the mosque while the women lay beautifully decorated tables with pies, samoosas, cakes, biscuits and sweetmeats. After the prayers the men go from house to house, wishing everyone well. At each house they are offered something to eat and drink. Children receive money as gifts at every house they visit. It is quite amusing to see them sitting down, counting their takings at the end of the day. Many a Tom, Dick and Harry become a Mogamat, Yusuf and Sedick for the day so that they, too, will receive money!

This is also the time of *Fitra* – a gift of a plate of food, or the eqiuvalent in money to a destitute Muslim. The name *Eid-ul-Fitr* derives from the word *Fitra*. At lunch time the family will gather around the table for the feast and to thank Allah for protecting them during the fast. Feasting and visiting friends then continue until late at night.

Basic soup

There isn't a great variety of soups in Cape Malay cuisine. The same basic recipe is used, and the soup is named after the thickening ingredient: peas, beans or lentils. Traditionally the fast is broken with a few dates and a sip of water, followed by a bowl of soup. Serves 6

Bean soup

Soak beans in water overnight. Place with all the ingredients in a saucepan and cover with water.

Bring to the boil, turn down heat and allow to simmer over low heat until the soup is thick and the meat falls off the bones. Remove bones but retain marrow and serve with ony-ony.

250 ml (1 cup) dried beans
1 kg (2¹/₄ lb) soup bones (shin)
3 carrots, grated
1 onion, chopped
1 tomato, peeled and chopped
3 turnips, grated
1 large potato, peeled and grated
250 ml (1 cup) each chopped celery and chopped parsley
6 allspice & 5 ml (1 tsp) peppercorns
10 ml (2 tsp) crushed garlic
salt and pepper to taste.

Curried mussel soup

Boil fresh mussels in water for 5 minutes. Remove from liquid and set aside. Retain liquid. Discard any mussels that have not opened.

In a large saucepan, sauté the onions in oil until soft. Add masala, turmeric, cumin and garlic to the onions and cook for 3 minutes over low heat. Add the mussel or chicken stock and crême fraiche and simmer until the soup has been reduced by half.

Return mussels to the soup. Season to taste and garnish with fresh coriander leaves.

2 kg (4¹/₂ lb) fresh mussels or 1 kg (2¹/₄ lb) cooked mussels on the half shell
2 onions, finely chopped
75 ml (¹/₃ cup) olive oil
5 ml (1 tsp) fragrant masala
5 ml (1 tsp) turmeric
2 ml (¹/₂ tsp) ground cumin
5 ml (1 tsp) crushed garlic
1,5 litres (6 cups) mussel liquid or weak chicken stock
250 ml (1 cup) crême fraiche
salt to taste
fresh coriander for garnishing

Ony-ony

250 ml (1 cup) cake flour
a pinch of salt
sufficient water to make a soft dough

Ony-ony may also be used for Boeber *to replace lokshen.*

Mix all the ingredients to form a soft dough that can be rolled out. Turn out onto a floured surface and roll out very thinly, about 2 mm (1/8 inch). Cut into long, thin strips and drop strips into boiling soup. When cooked, ony-ony has the consistency of boiled pasta.

Samoosas

The traditional filling for samoosas is beef mince, although a mixed vegetable, chicken or potato filling may be used with equal success (for beef filling, see page 77) Makes 36

CHICKEN FILLING

1 onion, finely chopped • 200 g (7 oz) minced chicken • 5 ml (1 tsp) ground cumin • 5 ml (1 tsp) ground coriander • a pinch chilli powder • 5 ml (1 tsp) crushed garlic • 5 ml (1 tsp) crushed root ginger salt to taste • 60 ml (4 tbsp) vegetable oil • 60 ml (4 tbsp) chopped coriander leaves

Stir-fry all the ingredients except coriander leaves in a saucepan until chicken is done. Remove from heat and add coriander leaves. Allow to cool before filling samoosas.

PUR

250 ml (1 cup) cold water • 5 ml (1 tsp) lemon juice • 750 ml (3 cups) flour • pinch of salt • vegetable oil for brushing • flour for dusting

Add lemon juice to water. Sift flour and salt, add water and lemon juice and mix into a fairly stiff dough. Divide dough into 12 equal portions, rolling each piece into a round ball (the size of a ping-pong ball).

Roll out each ball into a round disc about 6-8 cm (3 inches) in diameter. Place six discs on top of one another after lightly brushing both sides with oil, making sure that the entire disc is covered, and dusting the tops with flour.

The underside of the bottom disc and the top of uppermost disc must be left ungreased.

Repeat with remaining six discs. Roll each pile of discs into one large disc about the size of a dinner plate and place on baking tray. Bake in a hot oven (200°C/400°F) for 3-5 minutes to separate the layers. Allow to cool slightly and cut into strips 4 cm (2 inches) wide.

Pull layers apart and cover in a damp cloth. Fill and fold samoosas as follows:
• Cut a strip of pastry diagonally from A to B as illustrated (right).
• Bring A over to D by folding along BC.
• Hold onto C and bring B over to E by folding along CD, forming a pocket for the filling.

Place 10 ml (2 tsp) of cold filling into the pocket and bring F over to C, folding along DE, then fold along FE and tuck in the edges to form a triangle. Seal the edge with a paste of flour and water to prevent filling from spilling out and oil from seeping in when samoosa is fried.

Deep-fry samoosas in a large saucepan in hot oil until golden brown. Remove from oil with a slotted spoon and place on paper towel to drain excess oil.

Garnish with lemon wedges and serve warm.

FOLDING AND FILLING SAMOOSAS

ROTI

750 ml (3 cups) flour
5 ml (1 tsp) salt
50 ml (4 tbsp) vegetable oil
enough water to form a soft dough
250 g (9 oz) soft margarine
vegetable oil for frying

A flat, pancake-like bread usually served with curries. Small pieces are torn off with the fingers and used to scoop up the meat and sauces. Makes 18

Mix flour and salt in a large mixing bowl. Add oil and rub in with fingertips until the flour mixture resembles fine breadcrumbs. Add water and mix to make a fairly soft dough. Turn out onto a floured surface and roll out to the size of a swiss roll pan. Spread the dough with softened margarine and roll up like a swiss roll. Cover with a tea towel and allow to rest for at least 30 minutes. Break off pieces of dough and, rolling the dough between the palms of the hand, form into round balls the size of a tennis ball. Roll out each ball into a disc the size of a dinner plate. Fry in hot oil for 2 minutes on each side. Serve immediately with vegetable curry or mince curry.

SAVOURY VETKOEK

250 ml (1 cup) cake flour
5 ml (1 tsp) baking powder
a pinch of salt
5 ml (1 tsp) mixed herbs
1 egg, lightly beaten
125 ml (½ cup) milk
vegetable oil for deep frying

Vetkoek is delicious served with a savoury filling and ideal to send to neighbours during Ramadan. Makes 24

Sift flour, baking powder and salt together. Stir in mixed herbs.
Beat egg and milk together; add to dry ingredients mixing to form a soft dough. Heat oil in saucepan and drop dessertspoonfuls of the batter into oil. Deep fry until lightly browned on all sides and remove with a slotted spoon. Drain on a paper towel. Cut open and fill with chicken or mince filling for samoosas, mince curry or mini frikkadels.

Ramadan is a time of prayer and dedication

KEEMA AND RICE CAPSICUM

Use yellow or red peppers when available for an interesting colour combination. Makes 6

6 large green peppers • 1 large onion, chopped • 6 sprigs fresh coriander, chopped • 3 sprigs fresh mint, chopped • 1 green chilli, chopped 10 ml (2 tsp) crushed garlic • 5 ml (1 tsp) crushed root ginger • 10 ml (2 tsp) masala • 375 ml (1½ cups) cooked rice • salt to taste • 500 g (18 oz) beef mince, cooked • 125 ml (½ cup) vegetable oil • 2 large tomatoes, sliced 4 eggs, boiled and shelled • fresh coriander leaves for garnishing

Cut lids off peppers, scoop out the seeds and set aside. Add onion, coriander, mint, chilli, garlic, ginger, masala, rice and salt to mince and mix well. Fill peppers with this mixture. Heat oil in a saucepan and place stuffed peppers and tomato slices in the oil. Reduce heat, cover saucepan with a tightly-fitting lid and simmer over low heat until cooked through. Halve eggs and arrange in the saucepan. Cook for 3 minutes. Garnish with coriander leaves before serving.

PURI

Deep-fried puffs of dough served as a bread with curries. They can also be served as a snack with a variety of dips. Makes 24

Mix flour and salt. Add oil and rub in with fingertips until the mixture resembles fine breadcrumbs. Add enough water to form a stiff dough. Roll out very thinly (2 mm/⅛ inch) and cut into squares.

Deep-fry in oil until puffed and a pale golden colour. Serve with curry instead of rice.

250 ml (1 cup) flour
5 ml (1 tsp) salt
30 ml (2 tbsp) vegetable oil
water to form a stiff dough
vegetable oil for deep frying

SAVOURY SWEETCORN PUFFS

Quick and easy to make, either for the family or for unexpected guests. For a sweet variation, replace the pepper, chilli powder and Worcester sauce with a little sugar and top with honey or jam. Makes 12

Mix together egg, flour, salt, pepper and chilli powder. Add sweetcorn and Worcester sauce. Allow to stand for 30 minutes.

Heat oil and fry dessertspoonfuls of batter on both sides until golden brown. Top with any savoury topping (grated cheese, savoury mince or diced, cooked chicken).

If you are serving the sweetcorn puffs as a sweet snack, top with honey or blackcurrant jam.

1 egg, beaten
60 ml (4 tbsp) self-raising flour
a pinch of salt
1 can (410 g/¼ oz) sweetcorn, drained
a pinch of pepper
a pinch of chilli powder
5 ml (1 tsp) Worcester sauce
vegetable oil for shallow frying

A hadji *returning from Mecca, wearing an elaborately gold-embroidered* medora

BOEBER

A milk pudding flavoured with cinnamon, cardamom, rosewater and almonds. You can use ony-ony instead of lokshen Serves 6

100 g (4 oz) butter • 250 ml (1 cup) lokshen • 2 cardamom pods
2 sticks cinnamon • 1 litre (4 cups) milk • 50 ml (4 tbsp) sago, soaked in milk • 10 ml (2 tsp) rosewater • sugar to taste • 250 ml (1 cup) sultanas • 100 g (4 oz) flaked almonds • ground cinnamon

Melt butter in a saucepan. Add lokshen, cardamom pods and cinnamon sticks and stir over low heat until lokshen is golden brown. Add milk and bring to the boil. Cook over low heat until lokshen is tender.

Add sago and cook, stirring all the time, until sago is transparent. Stir in rosewater, sugar, sultanas and almonds. Sprinkle with ground cinnamon and serve.

PAMPOENKOEKIES

Pumpkin fritters are always served during the fast and are quick and easy to make when unexpected guests arrive.
Makes 24

500 ml (2 cups) cooked pumpkin, mashed • 60 ml (¼ cup) flour
10 ml (2 tsp) baking powder • a pinch of salt • 1 or 2 eggs • vegetable oil for shallow frying • cinnamon sugar for sprinkling over

Mix together pumpkin, flour, baking powder and salt. Beat egg and add to pumpkin mixture to form a batter of dropping consistency. Heat oil in a pan and drop dessertspoonfuls of batter into the pan. Fry until golden brown on both sides. Cover liberally with cinnamon sugar and serve warm.

VARIATIONS
Instead of pumpkin, use sweet potato for sweet-potato fritters, mashed banana with 5 ml (1 tsp) lemon juice for banana fritters or 1 can (410 g/14 oz) pineapple pulp for pineapple fritters. For potato fritters, use mashed potato and increase the salt to 5 ml (1 tsp).

RICE AND CORN CAKES

250 ml (1 cup) flour
10 ml (2 tsp) baking powder
5 ml (1 tsp) salt
250 ml (1 cup) cooked rice
250 ml (1 cup) sweetcorn
1 egg, beaten & 45 ml (3 tbsp) milk
vegetable oil for shallow frying
sweet or savoury topping to taste

For variation, add a little sugar to the batter and top with any sweet topping of your choice, such as honey or cinnamon sugar. Makes 12

Sift together flour, baking powder and salt. Stir in the rice, corn and egg. Mix thoroughly. Add milk and stir. Heat oil in frying pan and drop dessertspoonfuls of the batter into the oil. Fry on both sides until golden brown. Lift out with a slotted spoon and drain on paper towel. Add sweet or savoury topping to taste and serve.

Dhaltjies

Deep-fried savoury bites made with chick-pea (channa) flour.
Makes 36

Mix all the dry ingredients, spices and spinach in a bowl. Add egg and enough water to form a soft batter. Mix thoroughly and allow batter to stand for 30 minutes.

Heat oil in a saucepan and deep-fry dessertspoonfuls of batter until golden brown. Make sure that the oil is not too hot, for the outside may burn before the inside is cooked.

Lift out with a slotted spoon and drain on paper towel. Serve warm.

750 ml (3 cups) chick-pea (channa) flour
250 ml (1 cup) self-raising flour
5 ml (1 tsp) salt & 5 ml (1 tsp) turmeric
10 ml (2 tsp) ground cumin
2,5 ml (½ tsp) chilli powder
10 ml (2 tsp) baking powder
5 ml (1 tsp) crushed garlic
5 ml (1 tsp) masala
2 onions & 2 green chillies, chopped
½ bunch spinach, washed and shredded
1 egg, lightly beaten
vegetable oil for deep frying
enough water to make a stiff batter

MOULOOD (RAMPIE-SNY)

Moulood is the celebration of the birthday of the Prophet Mohammed (PBUH). The Cape Malay community celebrate this festival in a unique way which dates back to the days of the slaves. The *Moulood* is conducted throughout the mosques in the Cape. On the afternoon of the 12th day of *Rabi-ul-Auwal* women and their daughters, dressed in their best, most colourful clothes, go to the nearest mosque. They carry with them beautiful, carved chopping boards and special knives with bone handles and, in some cases, silver blades. The wife of the *Imam* of the mosque, *Motjie Imam*, coordinates the celebrations. She makes sure that there are enough orange leaves, aromatic oils and biscuits and cakes for tea. In the mosque the women gather the orange leaves, cut them into strips and impregnate them with aromatic oils. The cuttings are covered in colourful wrappings to form sweet-smelling sachets or *rampies*.

While the *rampies* are prepared, poems and verses on facets of the life of the Prophet (PBUH) are recited. Tea and cakes are served during the ceremony. In the evening the men go to the mosque to listen to lectures on the life of the Prophet (PBUH), followed by recitals of poems in melodious tones, commemorating His life. During the recitals brass sprinklers of rosewater are passed around for sprinkling on the hands and the handkerchiefs, and at the same time the *rampies* prepared by the women are distributed to the congregation. Tea is served with cakes and biscuits, and each person receives a *barakat* of cakes and biscuits to take home.

The celebrations continue throughout the month with get-togethers arranged by special *Moulood* clubs whose only function is the recital of poems and praises in honour of the Prophet (PBUH).

Women and girls preparing rampies

QUICK SCONES

500 ml (2 cups) flour
a pinch of salt
20 ml (4 tsp) baking powder
15 ml (1 tbsp) sugar
60 ml (¼ cup) vegetable oil
1 large egg
125 ml (½ cup) milk
jam and fresh, whipped cream
for garnishing

Versatile scones with sweet or savoury toppings are ideal to send to the neighbours during Ramadan. Makes 36

Sift dry ingredients together. Pour oil into a small bowl, add egg and milk and beat thoroughly to blend. Make a hollow in the dry ingredients and pour in liquid. Quickly mix with a knife to form a soft dough. Turn out onto a floured surface and press out dough with the fingers to 35 mm (1½ inch) thickness. Cut out with a round biscuit cutter. Place on a greased baking sheet and bake at 200°C/400°F for 10 minutes. Allow to cool. Cut in half and spread with butter.

Place a teaspoonful of jam in the centre and pipe fresh whipped cream around the edge.

FLAPJACKS

375 ml (1½ cups) cake flour
30 ml (2 tbsp) sugar
10 ml (2 tsp) baking powder
45 ml (3 tbsp) vegetable oil
2 eggs
125 ml (½ cup) buttermilk
185 ml (¾ cup) milk

Decorated with jam and whipped cream, these sweet bites also make a lovely presentation plate. Makes 36

Place all the dry ingredients in a bowl and mix. In a separate bowl, beat together oil, eggs, buttermilk and milk. Add liquid to dry ingredients and mix until only just blended. Drop dessertspoonfuls onto a hot, greased pan. Cook until bubbles forming on the surface burst. Turn over and cook for 1 minute. Remove from pan and allow to cool.

Serve with jam and whipped cream.

APPLE AND BLACKCURRANT PANCAKES

Adding rice to the batter gives these pancakes an interesting texture while the apple and blackcurrantsauce provides colour. Makes 12

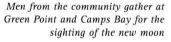

Men from the community gather at Green Point and Camps Bay for the sighting of the new moon

250 ml (1 cup) cooked rice • 250 ml (1 cup) milk • 1 egg, separated
200 ml (⅔ cup) self-raising flour, sifted • 15 ml (1 tbsp) sugar • 15 ml (1 tbsp) butter, melted • grated rind of 1 lemon • a pinch of salt
1 apple, peeled and grated • 2 ml (½ tsp) nutmeg • butter for frying

SAUCE
250 ml (1 cup) apple and blackcurrant juice • 10 ml (2 tsp) sugar
15 ml (1 tbsp) cornflour

Heat rice over low heat in 80 ml (⅓ cup) milk until all the milk has been absorbed. Remove from heat and beat in remaining milk and egg yolk. Add the rest of the ingredients except the egg white and mix well. Beat egg white until stiff and fold into batter. Heat some butter and fry dessertspoonfuls of the batter in a pan. When golden brown, turn and fry on the other side. Remove from pan and keep warm. To make sauce, place juice in a saucepan, add sugar and cornflour and cook until sauce is translucent. Pour over pancakes and serve.

Eid-ul-Adha

This feast is celebrated about 70 days after the end of Ramadan and at the completion of the pilgrimage to Mecca. As with *Eid-ul-Fitr* a lavish feast is prepared and children dressed in their best clothes go from door to door wishing everyone in the community well and receiving small gifts of money.

The holy pilgrimage to Mecca, or *Hadj*, is the last of the five pillars of Islam and is incumbent on every Muslim who can afford it. To undertake this sacred journey Muslims must be well prepared: they must have a good knowledge of the religion of Islam and live accordingly, they must be able to support themselves financially during the journey and still meet their financial commitments at home, they must clear up any ill feelings between themselves and others before they go, and last but not least, they must be mentally and physically strong.

Weeks before a pilgrim leaves for Mecca he or she goes around to family and friends to inform them of the departure date and to beg forgiveness for any hurt, real or imagined, which he or she may have caused. Pilgrims also ask everyone to pray that they will be able to complete the pilgrimage to the best of their ablity. Everyone is invited to the pilgrim's home for a meal or for tea and cake before he or she leaves. Each guest arrives with an envelope of money

(a *slavat*) which is handed over to the pilgrim. The completion of the pilgrimage is celebrated as *Eid-ul-Adha* which commemorates Allah's command to the Prophet Ebrahiem (Abraham) (AS) to sacrifice his son. Muslim families who have the means sacrifice an animal, usually a sheep, on the morning of Eid-ul-Adha. This ritual is known as *Korbaan*.

The animal must be free of all physical defects and the slaughter has to take place on Eid or the following three days. The meat of this animal is usually not eaten by the family, but distributed among the needy.

For many days after the pilgrims' return from Mecca, guests will call on them, enjoying a meal and listening to their stories about their experiences while they were on pilgrimage.

FRUITY BEEF CURRY

These beef-steak cubes simmered in a rich curry sauce are delicious served on a bed of pale yellow saffron rice. This is a popular dish to be served at Eid. *Use a good cut of meat for the best results. Serves 6*

Heat oil in a saucepan and fry onions, cloves, allspice and peppercorns until onions are lightly browned. Make a mixture of the vinegar, curry powder, masala, cumin, coriander, turmeric, garlic and ginger paste and brown sugar.

Rub into stewing steak until all the meat is well coated. Add the stewing steak and one bay leaf to the onion mixture and simmer over low heat until the meat is nearly tender and a thick gravy is formed.

Add apricots, close the saucepan with a tightly-fitting lid and simmer until the apricots are soft and the meat is tender.

Serve with Sweet saffron rice (*see* page 41).

50 ml (4 tbsp) vegetable oil
2 large onions, chopped
2 cloves & 3 allspice
1 ml (¼ tsp) peppercorns
125 ml (½ cup) brown vinegar
10 ml (2 tsp) curry powder
5 ml (1 tsp) masala
5 ml (1 tsp) ground cumin
5 ml (1 tsp) ground coriander
1 ml (¼ tsp) turmeric
10 ml (2 tsp) garlic & ginger paste
50 ml (4 tbsp) brown sugar
750 g (1½ lb) stewing steak, cubed
250 ml (1 cup) dried apricots
salt to taste

CHICKEN BERYANI

4 x 250 ml (4 cups) basmati rice
1 stick cassia & 2 cardamom pods
salt to taste
250 ml (1 cup) brown lentils
2 onions, thinly sliced
250 ml (1 cup) vegetable oil
4 potatoes, peeled and halved
1 kg (2¼ lb) chicken pieces
125 g (4 oz) butter
250 m (1 cup) water
a generous pinch of saffron
MARINADE
500 ml (2 cups) natural yoghurt
1 can (410g/14oz) chopped tomatoes
2 sticks cinnamon, 4 allspice, 6 cloves
15 ml (3 tsp) ground cumin
10 ml (2 tsp) ground coriander
5 ml (1 tsp) turmeric
5 ml (1 tsp) crushed root ginger
10 ml (2 tsp) crushed garlic
30 ml (2 tbsp) masala & salt to taste

Originally a Mogul-Indian dish, beryani will be served at just about any festive occasion. Make with fragrant basmati rice for the best result. Serves 6-8

Boil rice, cassia, cardamom and salt in sufficient water to cover. Drain and set aside. Boil lentils in sufficient salted water to cover until almost soft. Drain and set aside.

Fry onions in oil until golden, remove with slotted spoon and set aside. Fry potatoes in the same oil until golden brown, remove with slotted spoon and set aside.

Wash chicken and place in a large bowl with half the fried onions Make the marinade and cover chicken pieces with marinade. Leave for at least one hour.

Pour oil used for frying into a large saucepan. Sprinkle 500 ml (2 cups) rice over oil, then arrange chicken in marinade over rice. Layer lentils, potatoes and the rest of the rice over the meat.

Arrange the remaining onions over the rice and sprinkle saffron over. Dot with butter, pour water over and close saucepan with a tightly-fitting lid.

Cook for 10 minutes over high heat, then reduce heat and simmer for 1 hour or until chicken is tender. Serve with *Dhai* (*see* page 78)

Ghiema curry

Ghiema is beef or mutton cut into very small pieces, slightly larger than minced meat. For variation, add cubed potatoes and a chopped chilli. Serves 6-8

Sauté onions in oil until golden. Add ginger and garlic and fry for 5 minutes. Add tomatoes and spices and cook until a thick sauce is formed.

Wash the meat, drain and add to the curry sauce. Season with salt, close with a tightly-fitting lid and cook over low heat until the meat is tender (about 40 minutes). Serve with *roti* and sambals.

2 large onions, chopped
90 ml (6 tbsp) vegetable oil
5 ml (1 tsp) crushed root ginger
3 ripe tomatoes, skinned and chopped
10 ml (2 tsp) crushed garlic
15 ml (1 tbsp) masala
5 ml (1 tsp) turmeric & 2 sticks cassia
10 ml (2 tsp) ground fennel
1 kg (2¼ lb) ghiema
salt to taste

Fish frikkadels

Finely chop or mince the fish before adding the other ingredients if you do not have a food processor. Makes 24

Remove skin and bones from fish. Squeeze water out of bread. Place all the ingredients in a food processor and blend until thoroughly mixed. Form balls the size of golf balls and flatten them slightly between the palms of the hand.

Heat the oil in a pan and fry the frikkadels over medium heat until golden brown. Garnish with chopped parsley and serve with blatjang or sambals.

1 kg (2¼ lb) hake
6-8 slices white bread soaked in water
1 small onion, finely chopped
5 ml (1 tsp) crushed garlic
1 egg, beaten
60 ml (4 tbsp) chopped parsley
2 ml (½ tsp) nutmeg
salt and white pepper to taste
vegetable oil for shallow frying
chopped parsley for garnishing

Gestampte snoek

This paté-like spread is also known as snoek paste or snoek sambal and is delicious on freshly baked bread.

Remove bones from snoek and flake. Place in a food processor and add garlic, chilli and butter. Process until smooth. Add lemon juice with the blade running. Spoon into a small glass bowl and serve.

1 kg (2¼ lb) wind-dried snoek
1 clove garlic & 1 green chilli
100 g (4 oz) butter
30 ml (2 tbsp) lemon juice

Curried egg and rice bites

125 ml (½ cup) cooked jasmine-flavoured rice • 6 hard-boiled eggs, shelled and chopped • 60 ml (4 tbsp) fresh white breadcrumbs 125 ml (½ cup) grated cheddar cheese • 45 ml (3 tbsp) parsley, finely chopped • 5 ml (1 tsp) masala • 5 ml (1 tsp) salt • 1 egg, separated 45 ml (3 tbsp) dried breadcrumbs • 75 ml (5 tbsp) vegetable oil chopped parsley for garnishing

Mix rice, chopped eggs, fresh breadcrumbs, cheese, parsley and masala in a bowl. Add salt and egg-yolk and combine thoroughly. With floured hands, form small, round shapes. Brush with lightly-beaten egg white and roll in dried breadcrumbs. Heat oil in a pan and fry for 6-8 minutes until golden brown on all sides. Garnish with chopped parsley.

MERANG

This religious ceremony, still practised today, was part of the fabric of life of the slave community 300 years ago. While slave owners would gather for church services or *nagmaal* (communion), their slaves got together to learn to read and write and to practise and propagate their religion of Islam.

These gatherings were usually accompanied by elaborate feasting on food the masters did not eat: sheep or ox trotters, tripe, sheep heads, sheep tongues and the like.

Members of the slave community who could not attend received a *barakat*, or gift, in the form of special dishes of food delivered to them. These gatherings strengthened the slaves' feeling of community and gave them an opportunity to legitimately practise their religion, breaking their bondage for a short while.

Today people still get together for *Merang* on Sundays. After the prayers have been said the men sit in *safs* (rows) on elaborately decorated carpets on the floor. The food is served in bowls by the women and sent down the rows. Each person receives a plate and helps himself from the bowls. During the meal, the women keep the never-ending bowls of food warm and topped up.

The elderly women and children sit at tables in another room and are served while the men enjoy their meal. Serious, and sometimes heated, discussions take place during these meals, the topics ranging from politics to rugby and cricket.

Before the advent of the phone and the fax, attending *Merang* was a way of keeping in touch with the community.

After the meal *emmertee*, a very sweet tea made with condensed milk and sugar in a white enamel bucket, is served. Parcels of food or cake, the traditional *barakat*, are made up for guests to take home with them. The *barakat* still has a central role in the culture of the Cape Malays and to this day is considered a blessing.

BRAISED SHEEP TONGUES

6 sheep tongues
enough water to cover tongues
with 15 ml (1 tbsp) salt added
vegetable oil for frying
6 cloves & 6 allspice
4 bay leaves
salt and pepper to taste
SAUCE
125 ml (¹/₂ cup) brown sugar
5 ml (1 tsp) mustard powder
25 ml (2 tbsp) flour
25 ml (2 tbsp) lemon juice
25 ml (2 tbsp) white vinegar
1 ml (¹/₄ tsp) grated lemon peel
250–375 ml (1-1¹/₂ cups) water
125 ml (¹/₂ cup) pitted raisins

A highly sought-after delicacy for special occasions. Serves 6

Clean tongues, cutting off all the fibrous pieces at the back of each tongue. Lay in salt water overnight to remove slime. Heat oil in a saucepan, add cloves, bay leaves and allspice and fry for 3 minutes. Remove tongues from water and pat dry. Season with salt and pepper and fry with spices for 5 minutes on each side. Turn down heat, close saucepan with a tightly-fitting lid and simmer over low heat until tongues are tender. Serve with old-fashioned raisin sauce, saffron rice and sambals.

OLD FASHIONED RAISIN SAUCE
Mix the brown sugar, mustard powder and flour together. Add the rest of the ingredients, mix well and simmer in a saucepan, stirring continuously until thick. Cook for a further 5 minutes and serve with sheep's tongue or corned beef tongue.

PENSLAWAR

Curried tripe and baby onions in a thick, spicy sauce. Serves 6-8

1 kg (2¹/₄ lb) tripe • 15-20 small pickling onions • 10 ml (2 tsp) masala
10 ml (2 tsp) ground coriander • 10 ml (2 tsp) ground cumin • 5 ml
(1 tsp) turmeric • 10 ml (2 tsp) crushed garlic • 1 bay leaf • 3 allspice
3 cloves • 30 ml (2 tbsp) vegetable oil • 1 egg, lightly beaten
250 ml (1 cup) milk • juice of 1 lemon • salt to taste • ground nutmeg

Boil tripe in water with a little vinegar until tender. Cut into thin strips
and set aside. Sauté onions and spices except nutmeg in oil for a few
minutes. Add some stock from tripe to onions and bring to the boil over
low heat. Add tripe and cook for 5-10 minutes. Remove saucepan from
heat. Mix egg and milk; add to tripe, mixing well to prevent curdling.
Add lemon juice, salt and nutmeg to taste. Serve with yellow rice.

Food is eaten with the fingers of the right hand

GESMOORDE BREIN

*Braised sheep brains are still regarded as a great delicacy in the Cape
Malay community and will be served for special guests. Serves 4*

Remove brains from salted water and remove membranes. Fry onion in
oil until brown. Add brains and chilli and stir-fry for 6 minutes or until
cooked (opaque in colour). Serve with freshly baked bread and butter.

1 sheep brain, soaked in lightly salted
water overnight to remove blood
1 large onion, chopped
30 ml (2 tbsp) vegetable oil
1 green chilli, finely chopped

TROTTERS WITH ONIONS AND TOMATO

*These days you can buy pre-cleaned trotters and ask your butcher to
cut them into pieces. Serves 6*

Boil trotters in water, skimming off foam, until very soft and gelatinous. Place onions, allspice, cloves, peppercorns and water in a large
saucepan and bring to the boil. Cook until all the water has been
absorbed. Add oil and fry until onions are golden. Add garlic, chilli,
tomatoes, purée and trotters. Close saucepan with a tightly-fitting lid
and simmer for 20 minutes, stirring frequently to prevent burning. Add
more water if necessary.
    Add sugar to taste and season with salt and pepper. Serve with
freshly-cooked white rice.

6 sheep trotters, cleaned & cut into pieces
3 large onions, chopped
4 allspice & 6 cloves
2 ml (¹/₂ tsp) peppercorns
125 ml (¹/₂ cup) water
90 ml (6 tbsp) vegetable oil
15 ml (1 tbsp) crushed garlic
1 green chilli, chopped
1 can (410 g/14 oz) whole tomatoes
1 can (410 g/14 oz) tomato purée
sugar to taste
salt and freshly ground black pepper

TOMATO SMOORTJIE

Serve with frikkadels or any non-curry meat dish.

Heat oil in a saucepan. Add onions and sauté until soft. Add tomatoes,
chilli, cumin and garlic and simmer for 30 minutes to an hour adding
a little water if required.
    Add chopped coriander, season to taste and cook for 2 more
minutes. Garnish with coriander leaves and serve in a separate bowl.

60 ml (¹/₂ k) oil & 1 large onion, chopped
1 can (410 g/14 oz) chopped tomatoes
1 red chilli, finely chopped
5 ml (1 tsp) ground cumin
10 ml (2 tsp) garlic, crushed
1 bunch fresh coriander leaves, chopped
salt and sugar to taste

FRIKKADELS

45 ml (3 tbsp) butter or sunflower oil
1 medium onion, minced
or very finely chopped
10 ml (2 tsp) garlic, crushed
750 g (1½ lb) lean minced beef
1 thick slice crustless white bread,
soaked in water and squeezed dry
2 large eggs
5 ml (1 tsp) salt
1 ml (½ tsp) milled pepper
1 ml (½ tsp) ground allspice
75 ml (⅓ cup) chopped parsley

These meatballs are flavoured with spices which make them a real taste sensation. Traditionally served with tomato smoor. Makes 12

Heat 15 ml (3 tsp) of the butter, margarine or oil in a large frying pan and sauté the onion and garlic until transparent. Combine the onion with the mince, bread eggs, salt, pepper and allspice and shape into balls. Heat the remaining butter, margarine or oil in the frying pan and brown the frikkadels, a few at a time, for about 5 minutes on one side. Turn them over and brown the other side, then turn down the heat slightly and continue cooking the frikkadels for about 10 minutes, or until cooked through. Serve hot with mashed potatoes and an onion and tomato sauce.

CURRIED TROTTERS AND BEANS

*One ox trotter may be substituted for sheep trotters. You can
buy trotters pre-cleaned and ask your butcher to cut it into
pieces to reduce your preparation time.*
Serves 6

Boil trotters until soft and gelatinous. Fry onions, cardamom and cassia in oil until onions are golden.

Add tomatoes, spices, chilli and garlic and cook until the mixture is thick and mushy. Add cooked trotters and simmer for 10 minutes.

Drain beans and add to trotters. Add salt to taste and simmer until heated through.

Serve on a bed of freshly-cooked jasmine-flavoured or basmati rice with a selection of sambals.

6 sheep trotters, cleaned & cut into pieces
2 onions, chopped
2 cardamom pods & 3 sticks cassia
90 ml (6 tbsp) vegetable oil
3 tomatoes, chopped
10 ml (2 tsp) masala
5 ml (1 tsp) each ground cumin and
ground coriander
5 ml (1 tsp) turmeric
1 green chilli, chopped
10 ml (2 tsp) crushed garlic
2 cans (410 g/14 oz each) butter beans

GESMOORDE LONGETJIES

*Braised pluck is a special delicacy and very popular among Cape
Malays. Although it is hard work en time-consuming to clean and
prepare, it is well worth the effort. It is often served at a traditional
Merang. Serves 6*

Wash pluck and remove membranes. Soak in vinegar for at least 1 hour to remove blood. Pour off vinegar and clean thoroughly under cold running water.

Boil in water until tender. Cut into small cubes; set aside.

In a large saucepan, fry onions in oil with bay leaf, cloves, allspice and peppercorns until golden brown. Add pluck, tomatoes and chilli and cook for 10 minutes.

Add potatoes, salt and pepper to taste and close with a tightly-fitting lid. Simmer over low heat until potatoes are done.

Serve on a bed of rice.

1 kg (2¼ lb) pluck
vinegar for soaking
2 onions, chopped
90 ml (6 tbsp) vegetable oil
1 bay leaf
4 cloves & 4 allspice
2 ml (½ tsp) peppercorns
2 tomatoes, skinned and chopped
1 green chilli, chopped
6 potatoes, peeled and cubed
salt and pepper to taste

CURRIED CHICKEN WINGS WITH BUTTERBEANS

*Curried chicken wings served on their own also make a delicious cold
dish. Double-up the recipe and keep some in the fridge to serve later.
The delicious curry flavour is likely to improve even more.*
Serves 6

Wash chicken wings and pat dry. Mixed together ground spices and rub into chicken wings. Heat oil in a saucepan and brown chicken wings on all sides. Remove and set aside.

Sauté onions and garlic in the same oil until transparent, add chicken stock and bring to the boil.

Return wings and cook for about 15 minutes. Lower heat, add beans and simmer for 10 minutes with lid closed. Garnish with fresh coriander leaves and serve with rice.

500 g (18 oz) chicken wings
5 ml (1 tsp) ground ginger
10 ml (2 tsp) ground coriander
3 ml (½ tsp) black pepper
10 ml (2 tsp) masala
45 ml (3 tbsp) vegetable oil
375 ml (1½ cups) finely chopped onion
2 cloves garlic, crushed
500 ml (2 cups) chicken stock
2 cans (410 g/14 oz each) butter beans,
drained
salt to taste
fresh coriander leaves for garnishing

Old-fashioned bean and chop curry

250 g (9 oz) butter beans
30 ml (2 tbsp) vegetable oil
1 large onion, chopped
2 bay leaves, 2 allspice & 2 cloves
2 ml (1/2 tsp) peppercorns
5 ml (1 tsp) each masala
and ground cumin
5 ml (1 tsp) ground coriander
2 ml (1/2 tsp) turmeric
10 ml (2 tsp) crushed garlic
5 ml (1 tsp) crushed root ginger
250 ml (1 cup) brown vinegar
sugar and salt to taste
1 kg (2 1/4 lb) lamb chops

Lamb chops smothered in a delicious sweet-and-sour gravy with an irresistible combination of flavours.
Serves 6

Soak beans in water overnight. Add more water if required and boil until tender. Drain and set aside.

Heat oil in a saucepan and sauté onions, bay leaves, allspice, cloves and peppercorns until onions are transparent.

Add masala, cumin, coriander, turmeric, garlic and ginger and stir-fry for 3 minutes. Add vinegar, salt and sugar to taste (try to achieve a good sweet/sour balance).

Add lamb chops, close with a tightly-fitting lid and simmer until meat is tender.

Add beans and simmer until heated through. Serve with freshly-cooked rice and sambals.

Sweet and sour liver

750 g (28 oz) sheep livers, sliced
125 ml (1/2 cup) brown vinegar
3 cloves
2 ml (1/2 tsp) peppercorns
1 bay leaf
flour for coating
vegetable oil for frying
2 large onions, sliced
50 ml (4 tbsp) brown sugar
salt and pepper to taste

Not generally regarded as festive food, these liver slices are served in a delicious sweet-an-sour gravy. Even the most reluctant eater will enjoy them. Serves 6

Marinate lever slices in mixture of vinegar, cloves, peppercorns and bay leaf for 1 hour. Remove liver and set aside marinade.

Roll liver slices in flour. Shake off excess flour. Heat oil and fry liver until soft. Add marinade, onions, sugar, salt and pepper to frying pan and bring to the boil.

Stir well, making sure that all the cooking residue on the base of the pan is incorporated. Lower heat and simmer until a thick, golden-brown gravy is formed.

Serve on a bed of freshly-cooked rice with sambals or blatjang.

Sago pudding

375 ml (1 1/2 cups) sago
4 eggs, separated
2 sticks cinnamon
4 cardamom pods
180 ml (3/4 cup) sugar
10 ml (2 tsp) rosewater
a pinch of salt
500 ml (2 cups) milk
100 g (4 oz) butter
melted apricot jam for serving

Although many of the traditional desserts are vegetable-based, baked milk-puddings are also a popular choice among the Cape Malays. Rosewater gives ordinary sago pudding a delicate and unusual taste. Tapioca or vermicelli may be substituted for sago.
Serves 6

Soak sago in water for at least 1 hour. Mix together egg yolks, cinnamon, cardamom pods, sugar, rosewater, salt and milk. Beat egg whites until stiff and fold into milk mixture.

Stir in sago and spoon into a greased oven-proof dish. Dot with butter and bake at 170°C/350°F for 30 minutes or until firm.

Serve with melted apricot jam in a separate bowl (melt over low heat to prevent burning).

SWEET POTATO AND COCONUT PUDDING

Try not to add water when steaming the sweet potatoes. Serves 6

Melt butter in a saucepan and add cinnamon and cardamom pods. Add sweet potatoes in layers, sprinkling sugar over each layer. Turn down heat, close saucepan with a tightly-fitting lid and allow to steam over low heat for about 30-40 minutes. Try not to add water unless potatoes and sugar start burning, then add only a little at a time. Stir in coconut when sweet potatoes are soft. Garnish with cherries and mint leaves or shredded coconut and serve with custard.

100 g (4 oz) butter
2 sticks cinnamon
4 cardamom pods
1 kg (2¼ lb) sweet potatoes
250 ml (1 cup) brown sugar
250 ml (1 cup) desiccated coconut
cherries and mint leaves or shredded coconut for garnishing

EMMERTEE

This sweet tea is served in an enamel bucket at a traditional Merang. Guests serve themselves by dipping their cup into the bucket.

Place tea leaves and ground cardamom in the muslin bag and tie securely. Place bag in bucket and pour over boiling water. Add condensed milk and sugar to taste and stir to mix. Remove muslin bag when tea has desired strength. Serve after the meal at Merang.

250 ml (1 cup) tea leaves
15 ml (1 tbsp) ground cardamom
muslin bag
500 ml (2 cups) condensed milk
sugar to taste
sufficient boiling water to fill a
10-litre (18 pint) bucket

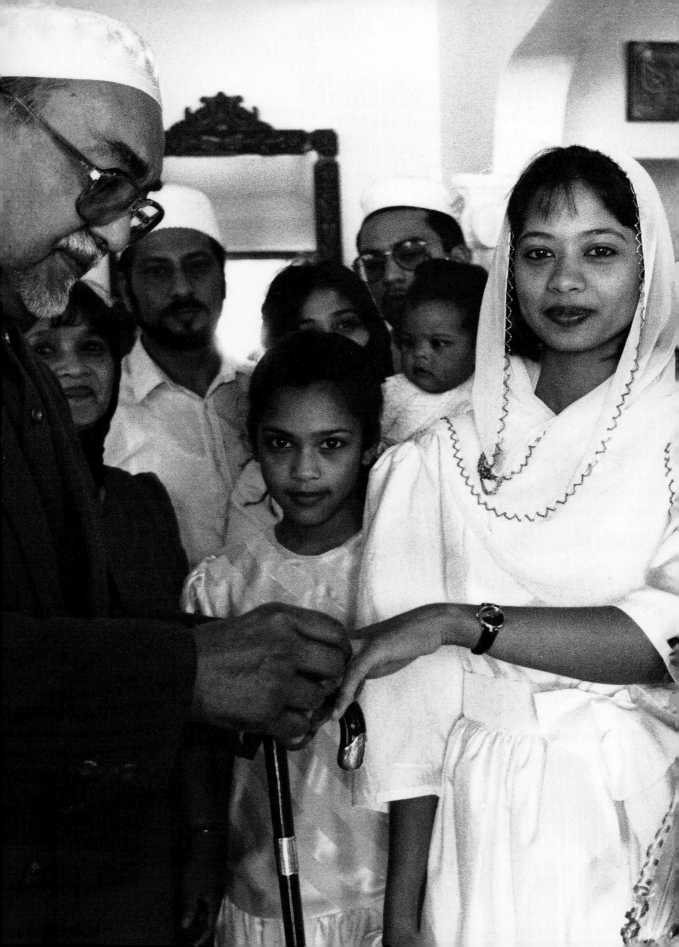

ENGAGEMENT

Unlike holy matrimony, marriage in Islam is a legal-social contract between a man and a woman. Contrary to popular belief that Islamic marriages among Cape Malays are arranged, a couple cannot be married without mutual consent. In the Cape Malay community the choice of a partner rests with the individuals concerned. Parents and elders do, of course, advise their children, and because of their wealth of experience there is often much wisdom in their advice.

Long courtships are discouraged. A young man has to ask the permission of a young woman's parents to court her. After a few visits, or when her parents deem it proper, they would ask the young man to send his parents (*ouers stuur*) to discuss marriage arrangements. If the young man feels he does not want to get married, he simply does not return to the young woman's house. If he is serious, however, he informs his parents of his intentions, purchases a ring, sets a date for the discussion and informs her parents of this date, which effectively becomes the engagement date.

For the engagement feast the young woman's family usually bake vast quantities of cakes and biscuits, arranged on exquisite glass platters, often bought especially for the occasion. These platters are wrapped in colourful cellophane and tied with beautiful bows. A tea table is set and the young woman's friends are invited to attend the feast.

The young man does not accompany the delegation who will discuss the engagement, but asks his father and elder male members of his family to perform this duty on his behalf. There could be up to 12 males in his delegation. They proceed to the parental home of the young woman, dressed in their best attire, bearing gifts and the engagement ring. There they are met by her parents where the young man's father informs them of his son's wish to marry their daughter. The message is relayed to the young woman who then formally agrees to the marriage, upon which the young man's father or one of his uncles places the engagement ring on her finger.

Now the wedding date is discussed, which in orthodox families may be as soon as a week after the engagement. The bridegroom-to-be does not take part in these discussions either, but stays at home with the female members of his family. After enjoying some refreshments the delegation leaves to inform the young man of the outcome of their discussions. Each member of the delegation receives a platter of cakes and biscuits to take home, while the celebration continues at the home of the bride-to-be. Most of the cakes and biscuits prepared for a *doopmaal* will grace the tables at an engagement feast. The following are firm favourites:

HERTZOGKOEKIES

Delicious coconut tartlets with an apricot jam filling.
Makes 24

PASTRY
425 ml (1³/4 cups) cake flour
10 ml (2 tsp) baking powder
10 ml (2 tsp) sugar
a pinch of salt
125 g (4 oz) butter
3 egg-yolks

FILLING
180 ml (³/4 cup) sugar
500 ml (2 cups) desiccated coconut
3 egg whites, stiffly beaten
100 ml (8 tbsp) smooth apricot jam

Sift together all the dry ingredients for the pastry. Rub in the butter until the mixture resembles breadcrumbs. Beat egg yolks and add to mixture to form a dough. Leave dough in refrigerator for 15 minutes then roll out to 5 mm (¹/4 inch) thickness on a floured surface. Press out rounds to fit into patty pans and line patty pans.

To make the filling, fold sugar and coconut into stiffly-beaten egg-whites. Place half a teaspoon of jam in the bottom of each lined patty pan and cover generously with coconut mixture. Bake for 15-20 minutes at 180°C/350°F.

SHORTBREAD

*Ground cardamom gives these ever-popular biscuits a special flavour.
Makes 24*

Cream butter and sugar until light and fluffy. Add remaining ingredients and mix to a soft dough. Press into a square biscuit tin and prick all over with a fork. Bake at 160°C/ 325°F until shortbread is just turning brown (40 minutes).

Cut into squares before it cools completely. Sprinkle with sifted icing sugar, loosen biscuits and cool on wire rack.

250 g (9 oz) unsalted butter
125 ml (1/2 cup) castor sugar
625 ml (2 1/2 cups) flour
125 ml (1/2 cup) cornflour
5 ml (1 tsp) baking powder
5 ml (1 tsp) vanilla essence or 3 ml
(1/2 tsp) ground cardamom
icing sugar for sprinkling on top

ROMANY CREAMS

These irresistible chocolate and coconut treats are even more addictive than their famous name-sakes. For the best results, use a good quality milk chocolate for the filling. Makes 48

Cream butter and castor sugar until light and fluffy. Add eggs one at a time, beating well to blend. Sift flour, cocoa, salt and baking powder and fold into butter mixture. Add coconut and mix to a stiff dough. Make walnut-size balls and place on a greased baking sheet. Press balls down with tines of a fork.

Bake at 180°C/350°F for 15 minutes. Loosen biscuits and cool.
Sandwich together with melted chocolate.

250 g (9 oz) butter
250 ml (1 cup) castor sugar
2 eggs
4 x 250 ml (4 cups) cake flour
ml (1/4 cup) cocoa
a pinch of salt
5 ml (1 tsp) baking powder
375 ml (1 1/2 cups) desiccated coconut
melted chocolate to sandwich
biscuits together

KOEKSISTERS

Traditional Cape Malay koeksisters are quite different from the plaited variety which forms part of the Afrikaner culinary heritage. The success of this recipe depends on the smoothness of the potato and flour mixture. Makes 36

Boil potatoes in water until soft. Drain and mash roughly. Add milk, oil, butter and egg and mash very finely, making sure there are absolutely no lumps.

Place yeast, sugar, flour, salt and all the spices in a large mixing bowl. Add mashed potato mixture and mix well to form a smooth dough. Cover dough with cling wrap and leave in a warm place to rise until doubled in volume (about 1 hour).

Knock down the dough and turn out onto a well-floured surface. Form into oblong shapes (60 mm/2 1/2 inch by 25 mm/1 inch) and allow to rise for 15 minutes.

Deep fry in hot oil until golden brown. Remove with a slotted spoon and drain on paper towel.

To make syrup, place all ingredients in a saucepan and bring to the boil. Stir over low heat until syrup forms a film on the spoon.

Dip koeksisters in hot syrup and sprinkle with coconut on all sides. Serve with coffee or tea.

6 medium potatoes, peeled and cubed
250 ml (1 cup) milk
60 ml (1/4 cup) vegetable oil
60 g (4 oz) butter, melted
1 large egg, lightly beaten
1 packet (10 ml/2 tsp) instant yeast
60 ml (1/4 cup) sugar
5 x 250 ml (5 cups) flour
5 ml (1 tsp) salt
7 ml (1 1/2 tsp) ground cinnamon
5 ml (1 tsp) ground ginger
2 ml (1/2 tsp) ground cloves
5 ml (1 tsp) ground naartjie peel
2 ml (1/2 tsp) ground cardamom
5 ml (1 tsp) whole aniseed
vegetable oil for deep frying
SYRUP
250 ml (1 cup) water
250 ml (1 cup) sugar
2 cardamom pods 1 stick cassia
desiccated coconut for sprinkling over

JOHNSON'S SPECIALS

4 eggs, separated
500 ml (2 cups) sugar
250 ml (1 cup) water
625 ml (2½ cups) flour
5 ml (1 tsp) baking powder
a pinch of salt
500 ml (2 cups) desiccated coconut
SYRUP
500 ml (2 cups) sugar
250 ml (1 cup) water
30 g (1 oz) butter
60 ml (¼ cup) cocoa
5 ml (1 tsp) vanilla essence

*The Cape Malays are fond of making Johnson's Specials (more commonly known as lemingtons) in various colours. Instead of cocoa, they will use food colouring and a little cornflour for the syrup.
Makes 24*

Beat egg yolks and add sugar a little at a time, beating well until mixture is light and creamy. Beat in water. Sift dry ingredients; fold into egg mixture. Beat egg whites until stiff and fold into batter. Pour batter into well-greased square baking tin. Bake at 180°C/350°F for 20 minutes. Turn out and allow to cool. Cut into squares.

To make the syrup, dissolve sugar in water over low heat. Add butter, cocoa and vanilla essence and bring to the boil. Remove from stove; allow to cool. Dip squares in syrup, coating well on all sides. Roll in coconut until liberally covered.

EASY LAYER CAKE

125 g (4 oz) butter
250 ml (1 cup) castor sugar
3 eggs
500 ml (2 cups) flour
20 ml (4 tsp) baking powder
a pinch of salt
125 ml (½ cup) milk mixed with
125 ml (½ cup) water
5 ml (1 tsp) vanilla essence
FOR VARIATION
glacé icing
whipped cream
fresh fruit or cherries and nuts

*This standard recipe can be varied by adding cocoa, spices, instant coffee or coconut for a different flavour each time.
Makes a standard layer cake*

Cream butter and sugar until light and fluffy. Add eggs one at a time, beating well to blend. Sift dry ingredients in a separate bowl. Add to egg mixture, alternating with the water and milk mixture, blending well each time.

Add vanilla essence and spoon into greased cake tins. Bake at 180°C/350°F for 20-25 minutes until well risen and firm to the touch or until a testing skewer comes out clean. Loosen sides and turn out onto a wire rack to cool. Sandwich the layers together with a filling of your choice and decorate to taste.

VARIATION: Make Fancies by using the same batter, but bake in a square tin (adjust baking time). Turn out and allow to cool. Cut into squares and decorate with glacé icing, whipped cream and fresh fruit or cherries and nuts.

PEANUT BUTTER COOKIES

250 ml (1 cup) sugar
250 g (9 oz) butter
45 ml (3 tbsp) peanut butter
625 ml (2½ cups) cake flour
500 ml (2 cups) desiccated coconut
500 ml (2 cups) each oats
and cornflakes
3 large eggs
7 ml (1½ tsp) bicarbonate of soda

*Crunchy peanut butter adds a lovely texture to these biscuits.
Makes 60*

Cream sugar, butter and peanut butter. Mix dry ingredients except the bicarbonate of soda in separate bowl. Beat eggs and bicarbonate of soda; add eggs to creamed butter and sugar. Mix well.

Add dry ingredients and mix to a stiff dough. Roll into walnut-size balls; place on greased baking sheet. Press down with the back of a spoon, leaving enough space between biscuits. Bake at 180°C/350°F for 15-20 minutes. Loosen biscuits and cool on a wire rack.

BANANA PURI

A good example of the Indian influence on Cape Malay cuisine, this recipe contains no bananas but the name comes from the banana shape of the fried puri. Makes 32

Sift together flour, salt and baking powder. Rub in ghee or butter until mixture resembles breadcrumbs. Mix milk and water, beat egg and add to milk mixture. Add to flour and mix to a stiff dough. Divide dough into six equal portions. Roll out each portion into a very thin disc the size of a small plate.

Brush both sides of each disc with ghee or melted butter and dust with flour. Stack the discs. Lightly roll out the stack of discs to the size of a dinner plate. Brush again with ghee or melted butter and roll up very tightly as you would a Swiss roll.

Cut into 10 mm (½ inch) slices. Press down each slice to about 10 mm (½ inch) thickness. Deep-fry slices in oil mixed with ghee over medium heat until rich ivory in colour. Lift out with a slotted spoon and drain on paper towel.

To make syrup, place sugar and water in a saucepan. Dissolve sugar over low heat. Bring to the boil and stir to thick, syrupy consistency. Add rose-water. Dip fried puri in syrup while syrup is still hot.

625 ml (2½ cups) flour
pinch of salt
2 ml (½ tsp) baking powder
20 ml (4 tsp) ghee or melted butter
125 ml (½ cup) milk
100 ml (8 tbsp) water
1 egg
ghee or melted butter for brushing
flour for dusting
SYRUP
375 ml (1½ cups) sugar
250 ml (1 cup) water
2 ml (½ tsp) rosewater

DIPS

Traditionally only tea and cakes were served at the engagement celebration. Today there is usually a variety of savoury snacks and dips as well. Deep-fried samoosa pur, puri or mini pappadums are firm favourites to be served with dips.

YOGHURT AND PEPPADEW DIP
500 ml (2 cups) thick Bulgarian yoghurt • 100 ml (8 tbsp) peppadew, finely chopped • 10 ml (1 tsp) crushed garlic • 5 ml (1 tsp) ground cumin • salt to taste • 1 red chilli, finely chopped, (optional)

Mix all ingredients together and serve as a dip with puri or crudités.

CORIANDER AND PARSLEY DIP
2 bunches of coriander, rinsed, with stems and roots removed 125 ml (½ cup) parsley • 5 large cloves garlic, peeled • 10 ml (2 tsp) ground cumin • 1 green chilli (optional) • 1 litre (4 cups) thick Bulgarian yoghurt • salt to taste

Place the coriander, parsley, garlic and chilli in a food processor. Process until finely chopped. Stir into yoghurt and season to taste. Serve with puri, fried pur or pappadums.

BILTONG PATÉ

200 g (7 oz) button mushrooms, thinly sliced
1 small onion, chopped
60 g (2 oz) butter
100 g (3 oz) finely grated biltong
250 g (8 oz) cream cheese
250 ml (1 cup) fresh cream, lightly whipped

With biltong so firmly rooted in the Afrikaner food tradition, it was only a matter of time for this delicacy to become part and parcel of Cape Malay cuisine. Serve with fresh bread.

Fry mushrooms and onions in butter until soft. Set aside and allow to cool completely.
   Place in a food processor with the rest of the ingredients and mix well. Garnish with watercress and wafer-thin slices of biltong.

CURRIED QUAILS EGGS

24 quails eggs (or 12 chicken eggs)
salt to taste
2 large onions, sliced
5 cloves garlic, chopped
250 ml (1 cup) vinegar
125 ml (½ cup) water
10 ml (2 tsp) ground coriander
10 ml (2 tsp) ground cumin
15 ml (1 tbsp) masala
5 ml (1 tsp) turmeric
2 bay leaves, 4 allspice & 4 cloves
1 ml (¼ t) peppercorns

These hard-boiled eggs in a sweet-sour curry sauce were traditionally made with penguin or chicken eggs. Today we have a thriving quail industry and quail eggs are available at most supermarkets. They are delicious in a fresh garden salad. Serves 6

Boil eggs in shells until hard, shell and set aside. Place the rest of the ingredients except sugar in a saucepan and bring to the boil.
   Turn down heat and simmer until onions are transparent but haven't lost their crunch. Add sugar to taste and stir to dissolve. Pour warm sauce over eggs.
   Allow to cool and store in a cool place.
   Serve with fresh bread and butter.

TOMATO SLAPHAKSKEENTJIES

A variation of traditional onion salad normally served in a mustard sauce. Serve as a snack on toothpicks.

Boil the onions in boiling salted water for 15 minutes, or until just tender. Drain, leave to cool, then remove the skins.

To make the sauce, combine the salt, tomato paste, cornflour and sugar in a bowl. Add the eggs and beat until creamy. Add the vinegar, beating constantly. Combine the milk and cream and beat into the tomato mixture. Add raisins and simmer over low heat, stirring constantly, until the mixture thickens. Remove from the stove immediately. Pour over the onions and leave to cool.

1 kg (2¼ lb) unpeeled pickling onions
SAUCE
5 ml (1 tsp) salt
10 ml (2 tsp) tomato paste
15 ml (1 tbsp) cornflour
125 ml (½ cup) sugar
3 large eggs, well beaten
125 ml (½ cup) brown vinegar
200 ml (¾ cup) milk
250 ml (1 cup) cream
50 ml (4 tbsp) raisins

WEDDINGS

A traditional wedding is without doubt one of the most elaborate of all Cape Malay feasts.

The wedding date is set at the engagement, and preparations for the wedding start immediately. A large hall is booked, the members of both extended families are informed and the menu is proposed, revised and argued about for many weeks until it is finally set.

One of the most outstanding features of Cape Malay family life is the great emphasis placed on inter-group cooperation, so practically the entire community becomes involved in the preparation and helps to bear the cost of the wedding.

A few months before the wedding the bride and groom, dressed in their best clothes, go out separately to invite guests to the ceremony and reception. They go from house to house and issue a personal invitation. Everybody in each household they visit is invited. A week before the actual wedding date, guests are invited to the parental homes of the bride and the groom.

The *strykery* or 'ironing' also takes place a week before the wedding. A room in the house of the bride's parents is cleared, where the freshly ironed trousseau consisting of elaborately embroidered, hand-made bed linen, towels, negligé sets, etc is displayed.

Guests are invited to view the trousseau and at the same time place their gifts on display. (It's very difficult to give a cheap present if everyone can see what you've brought!)

The night before the wedding ceremony female members from the groom's home collect the trousseau and wedding gifts which are then packed into the cupboards of the lavishly prepared bridal chamber. Preparing the bridal chamber is the responsibility of the groom who commissions one of the many furniture craftsmen in the community to hand-make the bedroom furniture. The female members of his family decorate the room with the most elaborate and rich curtains, bedcovers and cushions. The lavishness of the bridal chamber attests the status of the groom's family.

Traditionally the ceremony, as well as the reception, takes place on a Sunday. The hall or room where the reception will be held is decorated the night before the wedding by the menfolk. This is known as the *trimmery*. These activities are accompanied by the singing of traditional *liedjies* or songs and the cracking of ribald jokes.

At midnight *Gesmoorde snoek* (braised snoek), Sugar-bean bredie, rice and sambals are served with copious quantities of sweet tea to keep the singing throats lubricated.

*Bridesmaids are an important part
of the bridal retinue*

While the men are occupied with the *trimmery* the women start cooking. Expert cooks in the family are requested to do the cooking, assisted by the younger women. Catering for a traditional Cape Malay wedding can be a logistic nightmare.

The bride and the groom have separate nuptial feasts to which each invites his or her own guests. But any person, including non-Muslims, who chooses to come is welcome. Weddings are therefore truly community affairs with any number of possible guests attending each feast. And the biggest disgrace for any family is if there is not enough food for the guests. *Die wind het gewaai …* is the phrase used in hushed whispers to describe such a disgrace (the wind blew past the mouth leaving nothing behind).

The marriage ceremony takes place at the mosque where the bride is represented by her father or an elderly male member of the family. Neither the bride nor any other women attend the ceremony where the bridegroom publicly declares his intention to marry the bride, and pays the bridal price.

At the conclusion of the ceremony all the men at the mosque are invited to the bride's home for a lavish tea and to congratulate the bride. The bride, dressed in her morning attire and accompanied by two attendants, is placed in front of a mirror to await the groom who arrives with all the men to place the ring on her finger and to pay tribute to her parents.

The mirror reflects the evil eye back to anyone who has come to congratulate the bride, but has bad intentions.

At the reception, which usually takes place in the afternoon, tea, cakes and fruit preserves are served at frequent intervals, followed by supper towards early evening. The bride does not partake of the food at the reception as special *bruidskos* (bridal food) is prepared by the groom's family. The bridal food is covered with elaborate cellophane wrappings and placed on the bridal table for the bride and the female members of her retinue.

The bridal retinue includes best men, bridesmaids, maids of honour, a page boy and a flower girl. They travel with the bridal couple from one feast to the other where they occupy a central position, usually on a stage, ensuring that they are continuously in public view. If the bride is affluent enough she may change outfits up to three times during the day's proceedings.

For months after the event the luxuriousness of her attire, her beauty and good fortune and the food will be the focal point of discussions in the community.

Selected elderly women who have been on pilgrimage to Mecca dress in satin and gold for weddings. After supper the bridegroom sends them to fetch his wife.

Amid tears and farewells to family and friends the bride is accompanied to the bridal chamber by these women as well as any other guests who wish to see the bridal chamber.

This chapter details some of the dishes that will grace the tables at a traditional Cape Malay wedding.

Mutton beryani

By far the most popular of all the beryanis, this will be served at the most elaborate festive occasions. Do not even consider making it without basmati rice and real saffron if you want to achieve spectacular results. Serves 6-8

Boil rice, cassia, cardamom and salt in sufficient water to cover. Drain and set aside. Boil lentils in sufficient salted water to cover until almost soft. Drain and set aside.

Fry onions in oil until golden, remove with slotted spoon and set aside. Fry potatoes in the same oil until golden brown, remove with slotted spoon and set aside.

Wash meat, place in a large bowl with half the fried onions. Combine all ingredients for marinade, add salt to taste and spoon over meat and onions. Leave for at least 1 hour for the flavours to develop.

Pour oil used for frying into a large saucepan. Sprinkle 500 ml (2 cups) rice over oil, then arrange meat in marinade over the rice. Layer lentils, potatoes and the rest of the rice over the meat. Layer remaining onions over potatoes and sprinkle saffron over.

Dot with butter, pour water over and close saucepan with tightly-fitting lid. Cook for 10 minutes over high heat, then reduce heat and simmer for 1 hour or until meat is tender. Serve with *Dhai*.

4 x 250 ml (4 cups) Basmati rice
1 stick cassia & 2 cardamom pods
salt to taste
250 ml (1 cup) brown lentils
2 onions, thinly sliced
250 ml (1 cup) vegetable oil
4 medium potatoes, peeled and halved
1 kg (2¼ lb) mutton
a generous pinch of saffron
125 g (4 oz) butter
250 ml (1 cup) water
MARINADE
500 ml (2 cups) natural yoghurt
1 can (410 g/14 oz) chopped tomatoes
2 sticks cinnamon, 4 allspice & 6 cloves
15 ml (1 tbsp) ground cumin
10 ml (2 tsp) ground coriander
5 ml (1 tsp) turmeric
5 ml (1 tsp) crushed root ginger
10 ml (2 tsp) crushed garlic
30 ml (2 tbsp) masala

Samoosas with beef mince filling

Make the pur according to the recipe on page 49. In addition to this traditional mince filling, diced vegetables or chicken (see recipe on page 49) is also popular. Makes 36

FILLING
Fry mince, spices and chilli in oil in a saucepan until the mince is cooked. Remove from heat. Add chopped onion and coriander leaves and mix well. Allow to cool before filling samoosas as described on page 49. Deep-fry samoosas in a large saucepan in hot oil until golden brown. Remove from oil with a slotted spoon and place on paper towel to drain excess oil. Garnish with lemon wedges and serve warm.

100 g (4 oz) beef mince
5 ml (1 tsp) crushed garlic
2 ml (½ tsp) ground ginger
5 ml (1 tsp) ground cumin
2 ml (½ tsp) ground black pepper
5 ml (1 tsp) ground coriander
3 ml (½ tsp) turmeric
1 green chilli, chopped & salt to taste
60 ml (¼ cup) vegetable oil
1 medium onion, chopped
fresh coriander leaves, chopped

Gesmoorde snoek

When using salted snoek, soak in water for at least 4 hours, changing the water at least twice. Serves 6

Fry the onion, garlic, cloves and allspice in oil until onion is lightly browned. Add the tomatoes and chillies and braise for 10 minutes. Add the potato cubes and simmer for 15 minutes or until potatoes are almost cooked. Flake snoek, taking care to remove all bones. Add flaked snoek and pepper and cook until potatoes are done.

Serve on a bed of rice with blatjang.

1 large onion, sliced
2 cloves garlic, chopped
2 cloves & 2 allspice
60 ml (4 tbsp) vegetable oil
2 large tomatoes, skinned and chopped
2 green chillies, finely chopped
6 medium potatoes, cubed
500 g (18 oz) smoked or salted snoek
freshly ground black pepper

If the bride is affluent enough, she may change up to three times during the day's proceedings

OLD-FASHIONED CHICKEN PIE

This pie is always a firm favourite with celebrating friends and family. Serves 6-8

PASTRY

750 ml (3 cups) flour • 5 ml (1 tsp) salt • 500 g (18 oz) margarine yolk of 1 egg • 15 ml (1 tbsp) vinegar • enough ice water to form a soft dough • 250 ml (1 cup) flour • 125 ml (1/2 cup) cornflour • 10 ml (2 tsp) cream of tartar

Sift 750 ml (3 cups) flour and salt. Cut margarine into 4 equal sized chunks and rub one quarter into flour until it resembles fine bread-crumbs. Allow the other three quarters of margarine to soften. Mix egg-yolk and vinegar and add some ice water.

Gradually add water mixture to flour, mixing carefully with a small knife. The dough must be very soft. Cover and rest in the fridge for at least 1 hour.

Mix 250 ml (1 cup) flour, cornflour and cream of tartar. Sprinkle a rolling surface with some of this mixture and roll out dough on this surface. Spread another quarter of margarine over the dough, sprinkle with some more flour mixture and fold the dough in thirds.

Allow to rest in the fridge for at least 1 hour. Repeat until you have used all the margarine and flour mixture.

Cover dough and refrigerate until required. Remove from fridge and roll out to 5 mm (1/4 inch) thickness.

FILLING

1 large chicken
1 large onion, chopped
1 bay leaf
1 ml (1/4 tsp) peppercorns
3 allspice & 3 cloves
salt and pepper to taste
enough water to cover chicken
100 ml (8 tbsp) sago soaked in cold water
1 egg yolk mixed with 25 ml (2 tbsp) lemon juice
4 hard-boiled eggs, sliced

Place chicken, onion and spices in a large saucepan. Cover with water and cook until meat is easily removed from bone. Remove skin and bones and cut meat into small pieces.

Return to stock and season to taste. Bring to the boil and add sago. Simmer over low heat until the sago is transparent. Add egg yolk and lemon juice and stir well to prevent curdling.

Spoon mixture into a pie dish lined with pastry. Layer slices of hard-boiled egg on top and cover with pastry. Decorate with pastry leaves. Brush evenly with beaten egg and bake in a hot oven (200°C/400°F) for 30-40 minutes until golden brown.

Cut into wedges and serve.

DHAI

An essential accompaniment for spicy meat dishes. No Beryani should be served without dhai.

250 ml (1 cup) natural yoghurt
5 ml (1 tsp) salt
5 ml (1 tsp) cumin seeds
2 ml (1/2 tsp) chopped green chilli
5 ml (1 tsp) crushed garlic
60 ml (4 tbsp) fresh coriander leaves, chopped

Place all ingredients except coriander leaves in a food processor or blender and mix well.

Add coriander, stir and allow to stand for 1 hour to thicken and for the flavours to develop. Serve with Beryani.

CREAMY CHICKEN CURRY

Cape Malay curries are spicy rather than hot. The combination of fennel and cumin seeds gives this curry a unique flavour.
Serves 6-8

Mix together masala, flour, salt and pepper. Coat the chicken with this mixture, shaking off any excess. Heat oil and butter in a saucepan and fry the chicken breasts on both sides until lightly browned. Remove the chicken and set aside.

Sauté the onions, cumin seeds, fennel seeds and bay leaf until the onion is soft and transparent. Chop the tomatoes and add to onion in the saucepan.

Add the masala, turmeric, garlic and green chillies. Cook until a thick sauce is formed. Return the chicken and simmer until the chicken is cooked through. Add the yoghurt and heat through. Do not bring to the boil, as the yoghurt will curdle.

Just before serving, sprinkle over the gharum masala and dhania.

1 kg (2¼ lb) filleted chicken breasts
15 ml (3 tsp) masala
125 ml (10 tbsp) flour
salt and pepper to taste
50 ml (3 tbsp) butter
25 ml (2 tbsp) vegetable oil
2 large onions, finely sliced
10 ml (2 tsp) each cumin & fennel seeds
1 bay leaf & 5 ml (1 tsp) crushed garlic
1 can (410 g/14 oz) whole tomatoes
10 ml (2 tsp) masala
5 ml (1 tsp) turmeric
2 green chillies, finely chopped
500 ml (2 cups) yoghurt
5 ml (1 tsp) gharum masala
½ bunch dhania, chopped

SMOORSNOEK BUNDLES

phyllo pastry
100 g (3 oz) butter, melted
cooked smoorsnoek (half the quantity
made using recipe on page 77)
TOASTED CUMIN CABBAGE
10 ml (2 tsp) oil
10 ml (2 tsp) cumin seeds
½ cabbage shredded
SOUR FIG AND BALSAMIC SAUCE
125 ml (½ cup) sour fig preserve
balsamic vinegar to taste

Mouth-watering smoorsnoek in phyllo pastry is best served on toasted cumin cabbage with a sour fig and balsamic sauce. Serves 6

Open the phyllo pastry. Place one sheet of phyllo on working surface (cover sheets you are not using with a damp cloth), cut into 4 equal squares of about 25 cm/10 inches. Brush each square with melted butter and place on top of each other to form a 16-point star. Place 1 tbsp smoorsnoek in the centre of the pastry and gather up the edges to form a parcel. Tie loosely with string and fluff up the pastry edges. Brush parcel with butter. Place on a greased baking tray. Repeat until required number is made. Bake at 180°C/350°F until golden brown.

TOASTED CUMIN CABBAGE
Heat oil in a pan; add the cumin seeds and fry until brown. Add the cabbage and stir-fry for 3 minutes over high heat

SOUR FIG AND BALSAMIC SAUCE
Mix enough balsamic vinegar into the sour figs to achieve a pleasant sweet-sour taste.

TO ASSEMBLE: Place about two tablespoons of cabbage on a plate. Place the snoek parcel on top and dribble the sauce around.

Place phyllo squares like this

BOBOTIE

A lovely blend of flavours accounts for the popularity of this well-known Cape Malay dish. Using ground mutton instead of beef will result in a coarser texture. Mutton mince should be browned with the onions before mixing it with the rest of the ingredients.
Serves 6-8

2 thick slices of stale white bread
15 ml (1 tbsp) vegetable oil
50 ml (4 tbsp) butter
2 large onions, chopped
800 g (1³/₄ lb) beef mince
3 cloves garlic, crushed
15 ml (1 tbsp) masala
5 ml (1 tsp) turmeric
10 ml (2 tsp) ground cumin
10 ml (2 tsp) ground coriander
3 cloves & 5 allspice
2 ml (¹/₂ tsp) peppercorns
125 ml (¹/₂ cup) sultanas
60 ml (¹/₄ cup) flaked almonds
25 ml (2 tbsp) chutney
salt and freshly ground black pepper
6-8 lemon leaves
250 ml (1 cup) milk & 2 eggs, beaten

Soak bread in 250-300 ml/1-1¹/₄ cups water. Fry onions in oil and butter until just transparent. Keep aside.

Place all other ingredients except bread, lemon leaves, milk and egg in a large bowl and mix. Add fried onions in oil to mixture.

Squeeze water from bread, add bread to meat and mix well. Spread in a greased ovenproof dish.

Roll lemon leaves into spikes and insert into the mixture. Bake at 180°C/350°F for 30 minutes. Substitute bay leaves for lemon leaves if you have difficulty finding lemon leaves, but then use only 2.

Lightly beat eggs and milk together and pour over meat. Bake until egg mixture has set.

Serve with yellow rice and blatjang.

DENNINGVLEIS

One of the oldest and most favoured Cape Malay recipes with the most exciting combination of spices.
Serves 8-10

3 large onions, sliced
25 ml (2 tbsp) vegetable oil
5 plump cloves garlic, crushed
5 allspice, 6 cloves & 2 bay leaves
1 green chilli, finely chopped
10 ml (2 tsp) freshly ground
black pepper
1 kg (2¹/₄ lb) fatty mutton
25 ml (2 tbsp) seedless tamarind
250 ml (1 cup) boiling water
5 ml (1 tsp) grated nutmeg
salt to taste

Fry onions in oil in a large saucepan until soft. Add garlic, allspice, cloves, bay leaves, chilli and pepper. Layer meat on top of onions.

Close saucepan with a tightly-fitting lid and allow to simmer for 30-40 minutes.

Soak tamarind in boiling water. Allow to cool. Pour through a sieve pressing all the juices through with a spoon. Pour tamarind liquid over meat and sprinkle with nutmeg. Season to taste and simmer for 10-15 minutes. Serve with freshly-cooked rice.

NAARTJIE, PRUNE AND ALMOND RICE

An exceptional blend of flavours makes this rice dish a special treat.
Serves 6

500 ml (2 cups) rice
2 sticks cinnamon
2 cardamom pods
1 piece of dried naartjie peel
1 ml (¹/₄ tsp) turmeric
1 litre (4 cups) water
5 ml (1 tsp) salt
60 ml (¹/₄ cup) sugar
100 ml (8 tbsp) prunes (pitted)
60 g (2 oz) flaked almonds
60 g (2 oz) butter

Place rice, cinnamon, cardamom, naartjie peel, turmeric and water in a large saucepan and bring to the boil. Add spices and salt, turn down the heat and simmer until the rice is cooked.

Pour rice into a colander and wash under cold running water until most of the loose turmeric is rinsed off. Return to saucepan and add sugar, prunes, flaked almonds and butter. Stir through and close saucepan with a tightly-fitting lid. Steam over low heat until the rice is warmed through. Serve with bobotie or plaatfrikkadelle.

Sosaties

1 kg (2¼ lb) leg of mutton
8 wooden skewers
vegetable oil for frying
MARINADE
3 medium onions, chopped
5 ml (1 tsp) crushed root ginger
10 ml (2 tsp) crushed garlic
2 bay leaves & 6 cloves
10 ml (2 tsp) turmeric
5 ml (1 tsp) peppercorns & 5 allspice
75 ml (⅓ cup) masala
10 ml (2 tsp) ground cumin
10 ml (2 tsp) ground coriander
50 ml (4 tbsp) brown sugar
375 ml (1½ cups) brown vinegar
10 ml (2 tsp) salt

These sosaties are delicious when roasted over hot coals. Beef cubes may be used instead of mutton, but use a prime cut such as rump for the best result. For variety, marinade dried apricots and sliced vegetables with the meat and thread between meat cubes. Makes 8

Wash meat thoroughly and cut into 2,5 cm/1 inch cubes. Place meat cubes in a large bowl with a lid.

Mix ingredients for marinade. Pour over meat and allow meat to marinate for at least 4 hours, preferably overnight.

Shake off excess marinade and onion from meat and thread meat cubes onto wooden skewers. Fry for 10 minutes on all sides and keep warm in a lidded dish to prevent them from drying out.

If you are roasting the sosaties over the coals, baste them frequently with the marinade and take care not to burn the outside.

Simmer marinade and onions for 10 minutes. Serve sosaties on a bed of freshly-cooked rice with sauce from marinade spooned over.

Mafrew

2 medium onions, chopped
60 ml (¼ cup) vegetable oil
250 ml (1 cup) chopped tomatoes
30 ml (2 tbsp) garlic & ginger paste
3-4 sticks cassia & 4 cardamom pods
10 ml (2 tsp) masala
10 ml (2 tsp) ground coriander
10 ml (2 tsp) ground cumin
10 ml (2 tsp) ground fennel
1 kg (2¼ lb) steak, cubed
4 medium potatoes, peeled and cubed

This unusual dish consists of cubed beef in a hot, spicy sauce. Extremely easy to make, its attraction lies in the unusual combination of spices. It is traditionally served on a bed of savoury rice. Serves 6-8

Brown onions in oil in a large saucepan, taking care not to burn them, since this causes a bitter taste. Add tomatoes, garlic and ginger and sauté for 1-2 minutes.

Add all the other spices and simmer for 5 minutes. Add the steak and braise over low heat until the steak is tender.

Add potatoes and salt to taste and simmer until potatoes are cooked.

Savoury rice

1 large onion, chopped
1 green pepper, chopped
1 red pepper, chopped
60 ml (4 tbsp) vegetable oil
750 ml (3 cups) rice
1,5 litres (6 cups) water
10 ml (2 tsp) salt
a pinch saffron
500 g (18 oz) frozen vegetables (diced carrots and peas recommended)
4 boiled eggs, shelled
parsley for garnishing

Traditionally served with Mafrew or any other curry at celebratory occasions, rice sautéd in oil with onions, then boiled with fresh or frozen vegetables tossed in before serving adds another dimension to the staple food of the Cape Malays. Serves 6-8

Make savoury rice in a large saucepan. Sauté onions and peppers in oil until soft. Add rice and stir well so that every grain of rice is covered with oil. Add water, salt and saffron.

Bring to the boil, turn down heat, cover with tightly-fitting lid and allow to simmer until all the water has been absorbed. Toss in vegetables with two forks. Close lid and allow mixture to heat through, taking care not to overcook the vegetables.

Spoon savoury rice onto a large platter, spoon Mafrew over and garnish with slices of boiled egg and chopped parsley.

CRAYFISH WITH A CREAMY CURRY SAUCE

Although not as abundantly available as years ago, crayfish remains a favourite dish for special occasions. Serves 6.

Prepare the crayfish. If you use live crayfish, put it in fresh water to drown. Keep a large saucepan of boiling salted water or stock ready. Place crayfish in liquid and cook for 6-10 minutes (20 minutes if frozen). Remove from water with a slotted spoon. Set crayfish on its back and cut open the tail on either side with a serrated knife. Loosen tail meat. Or lay crayfish on its stomach and cut open from head to tail. Remove gut. Crayfish can also be steamed in a pot with seawater. Make sure the pot is tightly sealed. The cooking time remains the same.

Keep crayfish warm. Sauté onions in butter until soft. Add garlic, masala, cumin and coriander and cook for 2 minutes. Add flour and stir to make a roux. Add fish stock stirring continuously to prevent lumps. Add cream and salt to taste. Place crayfish meat back in shell and serve with curry sauce on the side. Garnish with fresh coriander leaves

3 crayfish, cooked and halved lengthways
1 onion, finely chopped
100 g (3 oz) butter
5 ml (1 tsp) finely crushed garlic
5 ml (1 tsp) fragrant masala
2,5 ml (½ tsp) ground cumin
2,5 ml (½ tsp) ground coriander
45 ml (3 tbsp) flour
500 ml (2 cups) fish stock
250 ml (1 cup) cream
salt to taste
fresh coriander leaves for garnishing

HOT CRAYFISH CURRY

1 kg (2¼ lb) crayfish
1 large onion, finely chopped
60 ml (4 tbsp) vegetable oil
5 ml (1 tsp) cumin seeds
1 sprig curry leaves
10 ml (2 tsp) crushed garlic
1 can (410 g/14 oz) chopped tomatoes
10 ml (2 tsp) each ground cumin and
ground coriander
1 ml (¼ tsp) turmeric
5 ml (1 tsp) coarsely ground red chillies
juice of 1 lemon
60 ml (4 tbsp) chopped coriander leaves

A special dish often seen on the bridal table. The crayfish is kept in its shell to obtain maximum flavour. Don't discard the crayfish legs – they often have the most succulent bits of meat.
Serves 6

Cook and clean crayfish and break into pieces. Sauté onion in oil until transparent. Add cumin seeds, curry leaves and garlic and sauté until onions are golden.

Add tomatoes, ground cumin, coriander, turmeric and coarsely ground red chillies; cook until a thick sauce is formed.

Add crayfish and lemon juice; simmer until crayfish is heated through. Add salt to taste; simmer a few more minutes. Garnish with coriander and serve with on a bed of basmati rice with a selection of sambals (*see pages 38-39*).

TRIFLE

1 sponge cake
100 ml (8 tbsp) smooth apricot jam
1 pkt (80 g/3 oz) strawberry jelly
500 ml (2 cups) hot water
1 can (410 g/14 oz) peach halves, cubed
1 litre (4 cups) vanilla custard
250 ml (1 cup) cream, whipped
100 g (3 oz) walnuts, chopped
1 pkt (80 g/3 oz) jelly of your choice,
prepared according to directions on
packet and allowed to set
glacé cherries for garnishing

No sherry or liqueur may be added if served to Muslims as this would make the trifle haraam. Serves 6

Halve sponge cake horisontally and spread a thick layer of apricot jam over each half. Cut sponge cake into cubes. Place a layer of cake into the bottom of a glass serving bowl.

Dissolve strawberry jelly in hot water and allow to cool, but not to set. Pour a little jelly liquid over the cake in the bowl, ensuring that each piece of cake is soaked.

Place a layer of peach cubes onto the cake, followed by a layer of custard and a layer of whipped cream. Sprinkle nuts over cream.

Repeat as above until all the cake and nuts are used, ending with a layer of custard.

Cube set jelly and decorate trifle with jelly cubes. Decorate further with piped cream and glacé cherries around the edge of the trifle. Refrigerate until served.

Any number of guests can be expected at a Cape Malay wedding and it is a great shame if there is not enough space and food for everyone

Malva pudding

For an interesting variation, make individual servings in a large
muffin pan. Remember to adjust the baking time
Serves 6

Beat together the eggs until light and fluffy. Add the apricot jam and
beat well. Sift together flour, bicarbonate of soda and salt. In a
saucepan melt the butter and add the vinegar and milk. Fold the flour
and milk mixtures alternatively into the egg mixture and pour into a
greased baking tray. Bake at 180°C/ 350°F for 45 minutes or until a
knife inserted into the centre comes out clean.

   Place all ingredients for the sauce into a saucepan and stir over
moderate heat until the butter has melted and the sugar dissolved.
Pour sauce over hot pudding. Pierce the pudding with a skewer so that
the sauce can be absorbed. Garnish with fresh mint leaves and serve
hot or cold with cream or custard.

250 ml (1 cup) castor sugar
2 large eggs
15 ml (1 tbsp) smooth apricot jam
185 g (6 oz) cake flour
5 ml (1 tsp) bicarbonate of soda
2 ml (1/2 tsp) salt
30 ml (2 tbsp) butter
5 ml (1 tsp) white vinegar
125 ml (1/2 cup) milk
mint leaves for garnishing
SAUCE
250 ml (1 cup) cream
125 ml (1/2 cup) butter
125 ml (1/2 cup) sugar
125 ml (1/2 cup) water

POTATO PUDDING

3 large potatoes
75 g (3 oz) butter
125 ml (1/2 cup) sugar
5 ml (1 tsp) almond essence
1 litre (4 cups) milk
4 eggs, separated
60 ml (4 tbsp) flaked almonds
stewed fruit or fruit preserves

Vegetables are often the main ingredient in traditional Cape Malay desserts. Serves 6

Peel and cube potatoes and boil until done. Drain and mash while still hot. Add butter, sugar, almond essence and milk and mix well. Add lightly beaten egg yolks and mix. Beat egg whites until stiff and fold into potato mixture. Spoon into a greased oven-proof dish and bake at 180°C/ 350°F until firm and a skewer inserted in the centre comes out clean. Serve with stewed dried fruit or fruit preserves.

PRESERVES

BASIC SYRUP
For every 500 g (18 oz) of fruit:
500 g (18 oz) sugar
750 ml (3 cups) water
30 ml (2 tbsp) lemon juice
SOUR FIG PRESERVE
500 g (18 oz) sour figs
basic syrup
2 sticks cinnamon
sterilised jars for bottling

In the Cape Malay tradition preserves are served with tea and enjoyed on their own, like sweetmeats.

BASIC SYRUP: Place all ingredients in a saucepan. Stir over low heat until sugar has dissolved. Do not allow syrup to boil.

SOUR FIG PRESERVE: Soak figs in water overnight. Pull off hard outer skins and cut off tips. Make basic syrup and add cinnamon before it boils. Add figs and boil slowly until figs are tender and syrup is thick. Bottle in sterilised jars while still hot.

GREEN FIG KONFYT: Carefully grate off the peel of each fig and cut a cross into the blossom end. Soak figs in water and lime mixture overnight. Wash thoroughly to remove all traces of lime. Boil figs in water and bicarbonate of soda until tender; drain. Make basic syrup, add cinnamon and ginger, add figs. Boil slowly until syrup is thick and figs are shiny. Bottle in sterilised jars while still hot.

QUINCE KONFYT: Peel quinces and slice evenly. Boil in water and salt until tender. Drain carefully. Make basic syrup, add ginger and fruit. Boil slowly until quinces are translucent. Bottle in sterilised jars while still hot.

WATERMELON KONFYT: Remove green skin and pink flesh from watermelon. Cut white part into cubes. Prick with a fork. Dissolve lime and bicarbonate of soda in water and pour over watermelon. Cover with a plate to keep cubes submerged. Leave overnight. Wash thoroughly to remove all traces of lime. Boil in water until tender; drain. Make basic syrup, add ginger and watermelon and boil over low heat until watermelon is translucent. Bottle in sterilised jars while still hot.

KUMQUAT KONFYT: Place kumquats in a bowl and cover with boiling water. Allow to cool; drain. Repeat. Cut a cross into the bottom of each fruit. Place in saucepan, cover with boiling water and boil until the kumquats are tender. Drain, then gently squeeze pips from fruit. Make basic syrup, add fruit and boil over low heat until fruit is tender and translucent. Bottle in sterilised jars while still hot.

GREEN FIG KONFYT
500 g (18 oz) green figs
water to cover figs
75 ml (5 tbsp) slaked lime
5 ml (1 tsp) bicarbonate of soda
basic syrup
3 sticks cinnamon
3 pieces dried ginger
sterilised jars for bottling

QUINCE KONFYT
500 g (18 oz) quinces
water to cover quinces
45 ml (3 tbsp) salt
basic syrup
1 piece dried ginger

WATERMELON KONFYT
500 g (18 oz) watermelon
75 ml (5 tbsp) slaked lime
10 ml (2 tsp) bicarbonate of soda
water to cover watermelon
basic syrup
1 piece dried ginger

KUMQUAT KONFYT
500 g (18 oz) kumquats, not over-ripe
boiling water to cover fruit
basic syrup

FUNERALS

In the Cape Malay community the rites and rules prescribed by Islam are followed for most funerals. A Muslim who dies before sunset should be buried before sunset. If death occurs at the end of the day or after sunset, the burial should take place as early as possible the next day.

Before the introduction of the Group Areas Act and forced removals most Cape Malays lived in close-knit communities around the mosques. When anybody from the community died, someone was appointed to go from door to door informing everybody of his death and the time of the funeral. These days, with the Malay community scattered around the vast Cape Flats, this is done by telephone and by means of announcements at the mosques. Everybody who is notified of a death in the community usually takes whatever he or she can afford in the form of money or food to the house of the deceased to help offset costs incurred by the family.

A *toekamandi* prepares the body of the deceased for burial by ritual washing. The body is anointed with fragrant oils and wrapped in white linen cloth. If the deceased is male, a male *toekamandi* undertakes this task, whilst a female *toekamandi* would do so if the deceased is female. Passages from the Koran are recited while the body is being prepared for burialby the *toekamandi*.

Only the men go to the service at the mosque and to the graveside. At the mosque prayers are said for the dead. In earlier times the male mourners carried the body on a *katil* (bier) resting on their shoulders, first to the mosque and then to the cemetery. Today, because of the distance to the mosque and the cemeteries, hearses are generally used to transport the body.

All domestic activity comes to a standstill in the house of mourning. No fires may be lit nor may any cooking take place in the home of the deceased while the body is still in the house. For this reason food for the funeral meal is often prepared outside in the back-yard. Because a funeral is a community affair, the family of the deceased have to cater for large numbers. Depending on how well-known the deceased was there may be up to 3 000 mourners. Huge pots of *kifyaat* (funeral food) is cooked under the guidance of a *motjie-kok* who will consider it a great honour to offer her services to the mourning family. Funeral food consists of dishes such as Pea and Carrot Bredie, Mutton Curry, Sugar Bean Bredie, rice and sambals. The food is served when the men return from the cemetery.

On the third, seventh, fortieth and hundredth night after the death family and friends gather at the home of the deceased to recite passages from the Koran and chant prayers. At these gatherings tea is served, with biscuits, cakes and savoury titbits. Gedatmelk, sweetened milk with rose syrup, is served to lubricate the throats during the recitals.

PEA AND CARROT BREDIE

3 medium onions, sliced
3 cloves & 3 allspice
5 ml (1 tsp) peppercorns
250 ml (1 cup) water
50 ml (4 tbsp) vegetable oil
500 g (18 oz) mutton neck pieces
500 g (18 oz) frozen peas
500 g (18 oz) frozen carrots
(julienne strips)
1 green chilli, sliced
5 ml (1 tsp) nutmeg
25 ml (2 tbsp) chopped parsley
5 ml (1 tsp) sugar
salt and pepper to taste

You are unlikely to be served pea and carrot bredie anywhere but at a funeral. Many visitors have to be catered for and the meat is 'stretched' by the addition of peas and carrots.
Serves 6

Place onions, cloves, allspice, peppercorns and water in a large saucepan. Simmer until all the water has been absorbed. Add oil and fry gently until onions are golden brown.

Add 125 ml (½ cup) water and the wet meat to the onions. Close saucepan with a tightly-fitting lid and simmer gently until a thick gravy is formed.

Add peas, carrots, chilli, nutmeg, parsley and sugar. Replace lid and simmer until the meat is cooked and tender.

Season to taste and serve with Creamed garlic and spinach pap (*see* page 91) or rice with blatjang and a selection of sambals.

Sugar bean bredie

A popular Cape Malay dish, particularly for special occasions and cold winter evenings. Serves 6

Soak beans in water overnight. Drain and rinse in clean water. Place in a large saucepan, add enough water to cover the beans and bring to the boil. Cook for 20 minutes and drain in a colander. Return beans to saucepan, cover with fresh water and boil until soft but not mushy.

Wash meat and set aside. Place onions, allspice, cloves and water in a saucepan and cook until all the water has been absorbed. Add oil and sauté the onions for 10 minutes. Add washed meat and braise for 10 minutes. Add tomato, garlic and chilli and cook for 10 minutes. Now add cooked beans, close saucepan with a tightly-fitting lid and simmer over low heat until the meat is tender. The beans should be soft but still retain their shape. Season with salt and pepper and sprinkle with parsley. Serve with freshly cooked rice and Onion sambal (*see page 92*).

500 ml (2 cups) dried sugar beans
1 kg (2¼ lb) mutton knuckles
2 large onions, chopped
4 each allspice and cloves
125 ml (½ cup) water
60 ml (¼ cup) vegetable oil
1 tomato, chopped
10 ml (2 tsp) crushed garlic
1 green chilli, chopped
salt and pepper to taste
60 ml (4 tbsp) chopped parsley

Mutton curry

Mutton has been eaten in large quantities in the Cape since Jan van Riebeeck introduced sheep to the country. South Africa is renowned for its fine quality of mutton. Lamb may be used for this dish, but the cooking time will have to be reduced considerably.
Serves 6-8

Heat oil in a saucepan. Add onions, cardamom pods, cassia and cloves and sauté until the onions are transparent. Add meat and tomatoes and braise for 10 minutes.

Add the rest of the ingredients except potatoes and coriander leaves, close with a tightly-fitting lid and simmer until meat is just tender.

Add potatoes and cook until potatoes are done. Sprinkle with coriander leaves and serve with jasmine-flavoured rice or roti and a selection of sambals.

75 ml (5 tbsp) vegetable oil
2 large onions, chopped
2 cardamom pods, 3 sticks cassia & 4 cloves
1 kg (2¼ lb) mutton
1 large, ripe tomato, chopped
10 ml (2 tsp) each masala & ground cumin
5 ml (1 tsp) ground coriander
10 ml (2 tsp) ground fennel
2 ml (½ tsp) turmeric
10 ml (2 tsp) crushed garlic
5 ml (1 tsp) crushed root ginger
1 green chilli, chopped & salt to taste
6 small potatoes, peeled
60 ml (4 tbsp) chopped coriander leaves

Creamed garlic and spinach pap

Not a traditional Cape Malay dish, pap is the staple carbohydrate of black South Africans who traditionally combine it with spinach or marog (a spinach-like vegetable). It resembles polenta and is delicious served with bredie or stew. Serves 6

Boil water in a saucepan, add salt and mealie meal. Cover and cook over a low heat for 15 minutes, stirring continuously to prevent lumps.

Sauté spinach and garlic with oil in a pan and cook until the spinach has wilted and all the moisture evaporated. Stir spinach mixture into the pap and pour into a greased 20 x 24 cm/8 x10 inch baking tin. Allow to cool and cut into cubes. Reheat by grilling or frying in a pan with butter. Use sage or any fresh herbs of choice for garnishing.

750 ml (3 cups) boiling water
5 ml (1 tsp) salt
375 ml (1½ cups) mealie meal
30 ml (2 tbsp) olive or vegetable oil
1 bunch spinach, chopped
10 ml (tsp) creamed garlic

When a woman is burried, the grave is covered with a prayer rug while the body is lowered into the grave

ONION SAMBAL

Add one or two chopped chillies for a sharper flavour.

2 large onions, sliced • 60 ml (4 tbsp) coarse salt • 60 ml (¼ cup) brown vinegar • 30 ml (2 tbsp) smooth apricot jam • 60 ml (4 tbsp) chopped coriander leaves

Place onions in a bowl and sprinkle with salt. Gently rub the salt and onion together with the fingertips to remove all the bitter onion juice.

Wash thoroughly in a sieve under cold running water to remove the salt. Return to the bowl.

Mix vinegar and apricot jam and pour over onions. Sprinkle with coriander leaves and serve with any bredie.

SAVOURY PIES

These savoury pies are equally popular with a curry-mince or a chicken filling. Makes 36

CURRY MINCE FILLING
Prepare Mince curry according to recipe on page 42.

CHICKEN FILLING
Prepare Chicken filling according to recipe on page 49.

750 ml (3 cups) flour
5 ml (1 tsp) salt
500 g (18 oz) margarine
yolk of 1 egg
15 ml (1 tbsp) vinegar
enough ice water to form a soft dough
250 ml (1 cup) flour
125 ml (½ cup) cornflour
10 ml (2 tsp) cream of tartar

PASTRY
Sift 750 ml (3 cups) flour and salt. Cut margarine into 4 equal sized chunks and rub one quarter into flour until it resembles fine breadcrumbs. Allow the other three quarters of margarine to soften.

Mix egg-yolk and vinegar and add some ice water. Gradually add the water mixture to the flour, mixing carefully with a small knife. The dough must be very soft. Cover the dough and rest in the fridge for at least 1 hour. Mix 250 ml (1 cup) flour, cornflour and cream of tartar. Sprinkle a rolling surface with some of this mixture and roll out the dough on this surface.

Spread another quarter of margarine over the dough, sprinkle with some more flour mixture and fold the dough in thirds. Allow the dough to rest in the fridge for at least 1 hour. Repeat this process until all the margarine and flour mixture have been used.

Cover dough and refrigerate until required. Remove from fridge and leave at room temperature for a few minutes before rolling out.

Prepare filling according to recipes as indicated above. Roll out pastry to 5 mm (¼ inch) thickness and cut into squares. Place 15 ml (1 tbsp) filling in centre of each square and fold corners of pastry inward over filling so that they overlap.

Secure with cloves and brush pastry with beaten egg-yolk. Place on a greased baking sheet and bake at 200°C/400°F until a rich golden colour. Serve warm.

Coconut tart

This recipe is also suitable for coconut tartlets baked in muffin pans.
This recipe makes 1 big tart or 24 tartlets

PASTRY
Prepare flaky pastry according to recipe on page 32.

FILLING
Place all ingredients except egg in a saucepan and bring to the boil over low heat. Cook, stirring all the time, until coconut is transparent and soft. Remove from heat, allow to cool slightly and add egg, making sure that it does not curdle. Line a 25 cm (10 inch) pie dish with pastry. Spoon in filling. Cut left-over pastry into strips and plait. Place in a criss-cross pattern over filling, neatly finishing off edges. Brush pastry evenly with beaten egg-yolk. Bake at 200°C/400°F for 30 minutes or until rich golden-brown.

250 ml (1 cup) sugar
500 ml (2 cups) desiccated coconut
125 ml (½ cup) water
2 sticks cinnamon
2 cardamom pods
egg, lightly beaten

Call to prayer

BASIC SPONGE CAKE

For variation, replace 50 ml (4 tbsp) flour with cocoa and add 3 ml (1/2 tsp) baking powder, or add 10 ml (2 tsp) instant coffee to the water.

175 g (7 oz) soft margarine • 175 ml (3/4 cup) castor sugar • 3 eggs, beaten • 375 ml (1 1/2 cups) self-raising flour • a pinch of salt • 30 ml (2 tbsp) cold water • 5 ml (1 tsp) vanilla essence

Cream margarine and sugar until light and fluffy. Gradually add eggs; beat until thoroughly blended. Sift flour and salt into a separate bowl and gently fold into egg mixture with a metal spoon. Add water and vanilla essence and mix. The batter should have a soft dropping consistency. Spoon batter into greased cake tins and bake at 180°C/350°F until well risen and firm to the touch. Loosen edges and turn out onto a wire rack to cool. Sandwich together with a filling of your choice and decorate to taste.

HEALTHY CARROT CAKE

250 ml (1 cup) honey
250 ml (1 cup) oil & 3 eggs
375 ml (1 1/2 cups) whole-wheat flour
10 ml (2 tsp) baking powder
10 ml (2 tsp) cinnamon
5 ml (1 tsp) bicarbonate of soda
250 ml (1 cup) grated carrots
250 ml (1 cup) mashed banana
125 ml (1/2 cup) mixed nuts
(walnuts, almonds & peacan nuts)
5 ml (1 tsp) ginger
250 ml (1 cup) sultanas
ICING
500 ml (2 cups) icing sugar
3 ml (1/2 tsp) vanilla essence
125 g (1/2 cup) cream cheese
90 g (4 oz) butter
sunflower seeds for sprinkling over

Whole-wheat flour gives this cake an interesting texture and adds healthy fibre to the diet. For an even healthier, but deliciously moist version, omit the icing altogether and pour 250 ml (1 cup) orange juice over the cake while still warm.

Cream together honey, oil and eggs. Sift together flour, cinnamon and bicarbonate of soda.
Add the flour mixture and the rest of the ingredients to the honey and oil mixture.
Mix together and pour into a cake tin. Bake at 180°C/350°F for 50 minutes. Trun out an alow to cool on a wire rack.

ICING
Mix together butter and icing sugar. Add vanilla essence to cream cheese and mix well.
Blend the butter mixture and cream cheese mixture. Be careful not to over mix as it becomes very runny. Spread over the cooled carrot cake and sprinkle with sunflower seeds.

GEDATMELK

1 litre (4 cups) milk
5 ml (1 tsp) ground cardamom
5 ml (1 tsp) cinnamon
sugar to taste
5 ml (1 tsp) rose syrup

A sweet, milky drink served at prayer meetings following the funeral. Serves 6

Pour milk into a saucepan. Tie cardamom and cinnamon in a muslin bag; hang it in the milk. Stir in sugar; bring to the boil over low heat. Remove from heat; allow to stand for a few minutes to infuse. Remove muslin bag with spices and stir in rose syrup. Serve in small cups.

APPLE TARTLETS

Use 2 cans (410 g/14 oz each) pie apples for the filling if you are in a hurry. Makes 36

PASTRY
Prepare flaky pastry according to recipe on page 32.

FILLING
1 kg (2¼ lb) Granny Smith apples • 500 ml (2 cups) water • 250 ml (1 cup) castor sugar • 60 ml (¼ cup) seedless raisins • 2 sticks cinnamon

Peel and core apples. Place apples and water in a large saucepan and cook until apples are tender.

Add all the other ingredients and bring to the boil. Allow apple mixture to cool. Roll out puff pastry to 5 mm (¼ inch) thickness and cut into neat squares.

Place 10 ml (2 tsp) filling in the centre of each square. Fold the corners towards the centre over the filling so that they overlap. Brush with beaten egg-yolk.

Place tartlets on a greased baking sheet and bake at 180°C/350°F until they are crisp with a rich, creamy colour. Serve warm or cold.

The Kramat on Signal Hill was built on the grave of Tuan Ghaibe Shah

INDEX